THE COLLECTORS

◆ ◆

To Barb & Don —
Happy Collecting !

[signature]

OCTOBER 26, 1996
MEMORIAL COLISEUM
FORT WAYNE, INDIANA

THE COLLECTORS

Anecdotes and
Answers about Antiques
and Collectibles

By Bob Rau

*Foreword by
Dana Garrett*

A Companion
Volume to the Public
Television Series

GRAPHIC ARTS CENTER PUBLISHING COMPANY

International Standard Book Number *0-932575-98-6*
Library of Congress Number *88-82193*
© *MCMLXXXVIII* by Graphic Arts Center Publishing Company
P.O. Box 10306 • Portland, Oregon 97210 • *503/226-2402*
Editor-in-Chief • *Douglas A. Pfeiffer*
Associate Editor • *Jean Andrews*
Project Editor • *Karla Powell*
Designer • *Marra/Dean Associates*
Typographer • *Paul O. Giesey/Adcrafters*
Printer • *Dynagraphics, Inc.*
Bindery • *Lincoln & Allen*
Printed in the United States of America

*The jacket photograph and the antique and collectible photographs are © by
Edward Gowans. The on-location photographs are: © by Tim Fuller (pg. 15);
© by Steve Haisman (pgs. 17 bottom, 18, 19); © by Susan Climo (pg. 17 top);
© by Ellen Hansen (pg. 21); © by Greg Anderson (pgs. 16, 20).*

*Special thanks to Gayle Ryan and Pat Young, The Sellwood Peddler, Portland,
Oregon, for allowing the jacket photograph to be taken in their wonderful store.*

1 | Frontispiece: Pâté de verre lamp

CONTENTS

To all of our collector and dealer friends who share our enthusiasm. Without their warm encouragement and response, The Collectors *could never have been.*

Bob and Dana

FOREWORD

by Dana Garrett

The day I met Bob Rau, I didn't realize that chance meeting would change the course of my career—and indeed the course of my life. I just knew there was an immediate rapport with this very charming and knowledgeable gentleman. I was hosting a morning talk show, and our producer had booked him as a guest to speak on antiques and collectibles, Bob's favorite subject. In thinking about the interview in advance, I had decided it would be fun to see if I could fool him, so I placed a pretty little Tiffany-like vase on the coffee table right next to an authentic Tiffany lampshade. I was hoping to make the point that our viewers need to be careful about reproductions of valuable items. Of course, when Bob came into the studio, he made a beeline for the coffee table. Holding the lampshade carefully he exclaimed, "I have the base that matches this." I turned to him with a smile and said, "So do I." He then picked up the newer vase and immediately identified it as a fine but contemporary "look alike." He didn't demean it in the slightest (I liked that), and it marked the beginning of a friendship and a professional collaboration that has lasted for years.

A couple of years after that first meeting, I was doing some serious soul-searching about what I expected from my career. I wanted to do something that would allow me to work with live audiences and also have a lot of input into the project. Although I had interviewed a wide variety of people during the time I hosted the talk show—from Jack Anderson to Donny Osmond, Mary Martin to Don Ho—the person who stood out in my mind was Bob Rau. What impressed me so much was his warmth, his way with people. His approach seemed totally compatible with my own vision of what a good program could be.

I decided to simply pick up the phone and ask him if he'd like to discuss a concept I had for a television program. How lucky for me that he was just retiring from a long and successful career in the insurance industry. He said he would like to talk about it—and shortly thereafter the idea that would become *The Collectors* was launched. While television production is a complicated business that only looks easy after you've studied, practiced, and worked very hard at it, it didn't take long for Bob to absorb its subtleties. I'd been doing this for some ten years before Bob, but he took to it like the professional he is.

People often ask about all of the objects they see on *The Collectors* set. These are things that Bob and I brought to give the show that lived-in, cluttered-attic look. These include an old alligator doctor's bag that Bob has had for years, and a cluster of twenty postal boxes with glass and brass fronts from Orcas Island, Washington. There are a couple of old paintings—one of a crashing sea and another of a woman playing a grand piano. These were wedding gifts to my grandparents more than seventy-two years ago. They get such a thrill out of seeing their things on the show each week. Yes, they still watch—and at 93 and 95, they still enjoy the show.

One item people often ask about is our little cast iron Scotty dog. When we started the show, Bob brought "Scotty" to sit in the window alcove. I immediately fell in love with this little guy (Scotty, not Bob) with the painted eyes and perky expression.

Several months later, I was working at the office on Christmas Eve. I left my desk for just a few minutes, and when I returned, "Scotty" was sitting there with a big red ribbon around his neck. The note attached from Bob said, "He may be our mascot, but he's your Christmas present."

From that time on, "Scotty" has been mine to take care of. Of course, as collectors know, collections have a way of growing. About twenty-five more things with a Scotty motif have found their way to me over the past few years, including candy containers, an old toy wind-up dog, a couple of bookends, and even one Scotty that was carved at the Shaker community in Sabbathday Lake, Maine.

Bob Rau is a very special man. Aside from the fact that he knows and loves his subject, he is also personable, creative, and very, very talented. He has sought not only to acquire objects, but also the necessary knowledge and appreciation through detailed study. And now, because of *The Collectors* program, he has the opportunity to share that knowledge and enthusiasm with people all over the country.

This book is written in Bob's own speaking style. It's informal, friendly, and *personal*. You'll find many of his *personal* observations, anecdotes, and cautions. Through the pages of this book I'm sure you'll enjoy getting to know the Bob Rau I know.

INTRODUCTION

by Bob Rau

Collecting can be viewed as both an art and a science. Yet, however you choose to describe it, collecting is an endeavor masked by a variety of motives. The one most often attributed to it is greed. But was it greed that prompted ancient civilizations to surround themselves with the precious artifacts that have awed succeeding civilizations? The creation itself of the artifacts was not really greed, but a sort of declaration of mythic power. However, right down to the Pharaohs who tried to "take it with them," the amassing of these objects could be called greed.

Yet, greed is such a nasty word. As the dictionary defines it, it is "a rapacious desire for more than one needs or deserves." Maybe we can soften the term a bit by just calling it an advanced stage of acquisition. The emotional connotations that are implicit in being a collector often transcend pure acquisitiveness. With the ancient Egyptians, their possessions were an attempt to deny the transitory nature of man. In other cases, such as with immigrants, their possessions eased transition by providing a link with their heritage. Either way, we have not yet become too modern for collecting. Isn't it ironic, then, that we have found a thoroughly modern way—via mass communication—to unite these guardians of the past called collectors?

The innovative idea of a television show just for collectors was a meeting of many minds. If I were to start at the beginning, it would be when Dana Garrett, who was then cohost of the talk show, *AM Northwest,* invited me on the program as a guest. With her beauty and animation—and disposition to match—I knew that appearing with Dana would be a delight. And it was! Our twenty minutes of impromptu appraisals and general bantering flew by, and all I could think after I left was, "I'd like to do that again." Which I did—not only on later *AM Northwest* episodes, but also on other local programs. I had really caught the bug.

Almost three years after those first appearances, I heard from Dana again. In the interim, she had left *AM Northwest* and had an idea for a show for Oregon Public Broadcasting. That idea would become *The Collectors*. With a few close friends, we brainstormed over how best to put the program together—what it should encompass, what it should be called, and how we could convince Portland's KOAP-TV, our first-choice station, to produce the program. Coming up with a name for the show is something I recall very well. Suggestions ran from "The Search for Nostalgia" to "This Old Couch." How fortunate that we decided on *The Collectors,* because this name reflects not only the essence of the program but our audience as well. After all, where would we be without our audience?

We agreed that the show should have three segments. The first would be interviews with an expert collector. The second would be a general feature on some aspect of collecting. The third would be on-air appraisals with audience participation. Proposal in hand, we approached the folks at Oregon Public Broadcasting.

Since Dana had worked on various projects for O.P.B., the door was open to the office of Tom Doggett, Director of Programming. Tom listened enthusiastically to our idea and arranged for a meeting with O.P.B. Executive Director Jerry Appy to discuss the potential program. Jerry had a strong interest in antiques and collectibles, so the idea appealed to him personally. But while Dana was well known to him as a television personality, I was not. His first words to us were, "Dana, I know you and what you can do, but, Bob, who are you?" I realized he was right and even though the approach stung, I decided to employ the experience of thirty-four years of selling and "sell myself" to Jerry. It worked. He bought our idea (and me). Tom told us to put together a pilot program, which we did with the help of our imaginative early mentor, Director Bob O'Donnell.

We built a partial set in the studio and did some interview and feature segments. Then we planned our first live appraisal—only (wouldn't you know it?) we picked a day in January when there happened to be an impossible ice storm! Still, the show must go on, and go on it did. Although the inclement weather diminished the number of guests, those who made it to the station brought extra items to be appraised. As these were thrust into my hands, I struggled through my first attempt at appraising in the role of cohost of my own show, rather than as a guest on someone else's.

The overwhelming response to this first show—hundreds of phone calls, cards, and letters—reassured not only Dana and me but also the decision makers at the station as well that our instincts had been right. Needless to say, we got the go-ahead and spent the first season touring the Northwest to look for interesting antiques, collectibles, locations, and people. Our formula was working.

The Collectors continued to work as a popular local show for the next two and one-half years. About that time, Maynard Orme came on board as the new Executive Director. As soon as he viewed a couple of the shows, he said point-blank, "This show has national potential. Let's pursue it." So we did. Dana and Tom Doggett put together a presentation to be sent to the Public Broadcasting Service. A word of caution came to us that the decision to go national with a show was a deliberative process and we should not expect a hasty reply—but in only six days we received a glowing response.

I can't accurately chronicle our good fortune without mentioning the rest of our talented and hard-working crew who have helped make that "luck" stick. There are some thirty people on staff at Oregon Public Broadcasting, who contribute to the success of *The Collectors,* among them Jessica Mitchell and Susan Climo, our creative inside people. Yet when we travel, the staff is reduced to six. Our key word has always been teamwork.

The coproducing PBS station in other towns offers equipment, additional personnel, cooperation, and expertise. It goes without saying that we couldn't do it without them, and I want to extend thanks to the myriads of people who have been involved. Yet our own traveling crew are the ones I know best, and I would like to single them out for the praise they so richly deserve.

Jennifer Garber, our producer, has brought to us the balance we needed when it became apparent that Dana could not be both talent and sole producer. She is not only effective and efficient but also delightful in her vivacity. It is Jennifer who deals with the monumental logistics involved in taking the show on the road.

Ron Peterson, our director, is one of those rare individuals who can keep calm in a storm. I have seen him do this literally, so it is not just a figure of speech. Once, after hours of exacting preparation, we were all set to film on the deck of the *Sternwheeler Columbia*—except for the fact that the weather had the audacity to defy us. As the patter of raindrops turned into a deluge, Ron kept disaster at bay. At best, television is only hectic. At worst, it can create havoc. Either way, our director keeps it under control.

Our senior producer, Judy Peek, helps mold our ideas into camera-ready actions. It's one thing to envision, quite another to enact. It is people like Judy who help ease that transition.

What we present before the cameras would be dubious at best without our head camera person, Ellen Hansen. It has been said that you can't make a silk purse from a sow's ear. Speaking strictly of myself (and not the lovely Dana), Ellen has proved that saying wrong time and again.

Last but not least, there is Dana, who instigated my opportunity to have an exciting second career after retiring from another. Her enthusiasm, professionalism, patience, and charm have proved the reverse of another saying: You *can* teach an old dog new tricks.

I think I've just about covered the people who have made *The Collectors* show what it is. There are others, however, who have contributed to its exciting companion book, *The Collectors: Anecdotes and Answers about Antiques and Collectibles.*

You will note a chapter at the end called, "Potpourri." The inspiration for that chapter came from the longtime collaboration I maintained with Buck Hannon, who for many years wrote on the subject of antiques and collectibles. Ever diligent in his research, Buck always uncovered the story behind the story, which lends that special lure to collecting. His death was a great sadness to me; I only hope I've done justice to his memory by culling from his writing the best of our joint efforts.

Yet another successful collaborative effort was with my editor, Karla Powell. She had the uncanny ability to take my words and re-express them in a way that had me always remarking, "I wish I'd said it like that."

As you read these words, I hope you'll find them entertaining and informative. The aim is to blend anecdotes and useful tips. It is a book not only about collecting but about you—the collectors for whom both the show and the book are named.

ON LOCATION

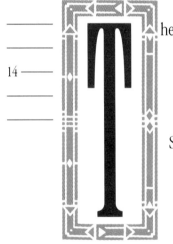

There are two things that are hard to predict—the weather and human nature. Both have caused us some problems on location, although I have *usually* found it easier to get around human nature. After all, people will respond to a smile, while the weather is quite impervious to anything I say or do. Yet, I can't help but notice how the elements often affect the human element.

Sisters is a historic little town located at the edge of the high desert country in Central Oregon, where temperatures soar in the middle of summer. We filmed there one mid-July day and had quite a time keeping Dana and me *looking* cool (although we certainly felt far from it). You know the saying that men sweat and women perspire? Well, Dana and I were on equal footing in that regard with the combination of the merciless sun and banks of blazing front lights. All the cool professionalism and powder in the world couldn't beat that kind of heat, but somehow our director and camera people managed to make us appear undaunted.

Apparently, I was a little *too* undaunted for one of our guests that day: in fact, I was told off. A gentleman brought a beautiful charger up to me, easily recognizable as a Mettlach. As I showed it to the audience and described what it was, the owner exclaimed, "Well, of course it's Mettlach. It's marked right on the back, and you're looking at it." Although he was quite indignant, everyone else got a big kick out of it, including me. I acknowledged his point, and he softened a little. "Well, you probably knew what it was anyway," he conceded. Although we deliberated over that scene when back in the editing room, we opted for some cinéma vérité and went

*Make-up and Western cos-
tumes add atmosphere and
meaning for a program
filmed in Tucson, Arizona.*

ahead and used the scene on the show. Blame it on the heat, but I still chuckle
every time I think of it.

Basically, I would categorize our guests as three types: First, those who know their item
and are just looking for confirmation. Second, those who haven't the faintest idea
what their item may be. Third, those who think they know but who really have
been misinformed.

When an object has been appraised skillfully, all I need to do is corroborate that
evaluation, which fits into the first category of guests. However, if the so-called
appraisal is really an offhand comment by a well-meaning neighbor or friend, then
I sometimes find myself in the tricky — even uncomfortable — role of dealing with
people in that last category. Perhaps a guest has been told by someone that her

Filming out-of-doors causes crew and cast to have to deal with ever-changing light, wind, and noise levels.

17

The studio audience participates with Bob during an appraisal on the set at Oregon Public Broadcasting.

Sometimes the object of everyone's attention requires special security, as with this rare Tiffany lamp.

beautiful lamp must be worth $2,000 because "my aunt had one just like it, and
she sold it for that much." Then she brings it to me on the show, and it is only too
obvious that it's just a nice overmetal lamp with slag panels, worth much less than
anticipated—and it's my job to keep our guest happy, yet stay honest.

Of course, when I appraise the lamp at $400 and the guest is expecting to hear $2,000,
obviously there will be disappointment. Unfortunately, the most common pitfall
with people seeking appraisals is: The higher the evaluation, the more credible the
evaluator. Generally, however, all it takes is a sincere, logical explanation to
change the frown to a smile. If we are able to discuss it, most people understand
what happened.

An example of how things can get lost in the translation is what I call the "my aunt
told me" syndrome. At one show a lady brought a piece of Fenton cranberry
hobnail with opaline hobs to be appraised. When asked what she knew about the
piece, she replied, "My aunt gave it to me, and she said it belonged to my great-
grandmother." Well, if it belonged to great-grandmother, she must have secured it
at the age of one hundred because the piece was circa 1930. Had it been the old
cranberry opaline hobnail circa 1890, we would have had both age and high value.
As it was, it was a good Fenton with a fair figure; but still a little disappointing to
our guest.

It is easy to understand how confusion arises over the assumed age of a piece. It all boils down to how old great-grandma was when she acquired the piece. A young lady may indeed have an heirloom that once belonged to great-grandma. But if great-grandma was a not-so-young lady when she bought it—well, it's just a matter of arithmetic.

On the other hand, guests without such expectations are almost always delighted to finally discover just what it is they've had all these years. For them, the value is purely subjective, and they leave satisfied. For us on *The Collectors,* the challenge is to keep our guests happy, regardless of their previous expectations. As long as they get what they came for—entertainment and information—then we can claim a job well done.

Sometimes, though, Dana and I get to indulge in a little whimsy as well, such as the time we were filming in Wisconsin. Our two main locations were the Experimental Aeronautical Association in Oshkosh and the Circus Museum in Baraboo. I had the privilege of living out my own personal Walter Mitty fantasy with the chance to soar in a Lincoln biplane. I donned aviator goggles, bomber jacket, and the obligatory white scarf, then put myself in the hands of an ace pilot. The only disturbing thing to me was that he was older than I, and believe me, that's disturbing. I found out later that he is an internationally renowned pilot with many years of experience in flying old aircraft.

A flying experiment of a different sort took place on the ground. As a unique opening to this particular segment of the show, Dana rode bareback on a full-grown circus elephant. Just as she was about to welcome our viewers to Wisconsin, the elephant decided to try to upstage her and rose on its hind legs. But Dana clung to her harness without missing a beat. All in all, this was quite a hair-raising (or in my case, *air*-raising) show opener.

Our producers are coming up with more of these on-location scene setters. It's all in the spirit of continually improving the show by adding in the humor and variety of the unexpected while retaining the original intent, which is sharing the pleasure and knowledge of being a collector.

A lot of people are casual collectors, be it for fun, profit, or nostalgia. In actual fact, everyone has *something* that is valuable to him or her personally and is cherished as a collectible—whether it is one item or ten thousand. That is collecting. But there is one common thread quite noticeable among serious collectors—they study hard and learn their lessons well. I would add to this that, if they collect for a profit, they probably "make money the old-fashioned way—they earn it."

It is always fascinating to me to see a collector develop the knowledge and skills needed to truly become an authority. You must be willing to start out slowly and let your knowledge and confidence grow. Learn both from other collectors and dealers as well as from your own study and experience. Let's take Fiesta ware as an example. *(Figure 3)*. While the pieces are not yet what could be called expensive, if you are going to put out $25 to $50 for a colorful bowl, you must have some real knowledge of what you are doing.

Every serious Fiesta ware collector I have ever met has learned the exact dates of manufacture and the years certain colors were created. He or she has studied to be able to trace the basic Fiesta ware designs through the years and has become knowledgeable on everything that must be known to be an authority. The experienced collector has learned to see the difference between the marks of impressed Fiesta ware and that with the black stamped signature.

You can find a number of books on Fiesta ware, along with guides to color, style, and pricing. You will be able to determine which colors cost a little bit more and which

2 | *French doll*

ones are older (as compared to the newer, pastel Fiesta ware). Some people will try to collect a whole set of one color, while others will mix and match so they can create a brilliant rainbow effect with their table setting. As you study more, you will realize that, although Fiesta ware was created in the Depression era, it has all the elegance of Art Deco.

Now that you have found out that hands-on study is a vital, indispensable part of collecting, you will enjoy going to shows, sales, and shops—where you'll be thrilled to find that extra cup in the exact style you wanted. By then you will know that there are two basic designs of cups. If you want to match an entire set, it will take some searching, but it will be worth it when you are able to set your table with the brilliance of a full matching set of Fiesta ware.

The question comes up often: Is there enough Fiesta ware still around to collect? Definitely so; the Homer Laughlin Company of Newell, West Virginia, turned out millions of pieces each year as late as the 1940s. Many mothers and grandmothers

had individual pieces, and some had sets. Its low cost and high accessibility made it a popular collectible even during those Depression years. It continues to be a popular collectible despite the changes in that original status.

Let's face it, glass and pottery can break. When a piece of Fiesta ware breaks or chips, it is quite obvious because it is such a colorful item. Here an inverse ratio comes into play: there are more and more Fiesta ware collectors and fewer and fewer intact older pieces available to collect. Also, prices have been increasing for years, and they continue to go up. Yet isn't it funny how collectors' enthusiasm rises right along with the prices?

Another wonder one finds in collecting is the span of time between relatively recent collectibles, such as Fiesta ware, and collectibles that can be traced back through the history of civilization. Dolls are an example of such a timeless item.

Let's say you want to get into doll collecting. You can find dolls ranging from $30 to $50; you can also find them ranging in the thousands of dollars. It is a fascinating study—actually a hobby in itself—to discover which dolls came from which countries. The more you know, the more you can appreciate both the elegance of a high-fashion French doll *(Figure 2)* and the homespun charm of the Kewpie doll *(Figure 4)*. Or perhaps you would like to know more about the collectibility and value of dolls marked "Made in Occupied Japan," and how they might compare in value to others simply marked "Made in Japan."

Whatever your interest, collecting offers admission to a fascinating world of nostalgia. But those who get involved in it should understand not only the beauty and the legacy of their favorite collectibles but also their present and potential value. As with collectors of Fiesta ware, I have yet to meet a doll collector who is not amazingly well-versed. There is simply no easy way to gain this kind of expertise; it is gained only by learning from other experts and by individual study.

Many collectors end up in the antique business just because they have accumulated so much. When they decide to sell, the obvious way is to go into business for themselves. That is all well and good, but when their own initial stock thins out, it is not so easy to replace it. This, in part, explains the rapid appreciation in the value of collectibles that so often occurs. When the collector-turned-dealer replenishes stock by buying from other collectors, the price has inflated. The dealer must mark up prices yet again to make the same margin of profit, and so it goes. As with many other endeavors, the collectors' marketplace is not always a natural one. Prices fluctuate according to the whim of the public's interest, not according to its needs. The scarcity, age, and beauty of an item are only part of the total picture; who once owned it or who might want it now can have a major influence on the fickle market of collectors.

Both greater quantity and better quality of many reproductions are proving to be a hindrance to the fair market value of the originals. It pays to be an expert when reproductions saturate the market.

One of my favorite stories about how nutty the business can get happened at the estate sale of a magnificent home. A friend of mine attended this event as a buyer, only to be enlisted by the owner to help out in the basement. It was sheer bedlam. Things were so hectic my friend didn't have time to determine where people were finding the curiously shaped pieces of wood she priced extemporaneously at the exit.

It wasn't until later in the day that she discovered, to her chagrin, that those strange wooden pieces were the workings of a huge pump organ. Even more amazing was the gentleman who came along at that moment and paid full price for the organ, knowing it was hollow. So my friend literally sold the organ twice—first the working parts and then the framework. Whether that was salesmanship or luck, it is still a prime example of what goes on with that lovable lot called "collectors."

It has been said that the only thing wrong with nostalgia is that there's no future in it. A cute comment, but untrue when it comes to the world of collecting. In that world, nostalgia *is* the future. Happy hunting!

4 \ Kewpie doll

MY INTRODUCTION TO COLLECTING

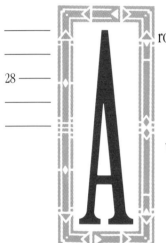

Around 1860, glassmakers in the United States began making a fashionable, as well as useful, form of tableware called the cruet. My own grandma's round oak table always had a vinegar cruet placed right in the middle of it. The cruet was pressed glass, had a stopper, and was a treasure to her. It became as much of a treasure to me, and indeed became my first love in collectibles.

When I began my dalliance with glass collecting, it was not uncommon to pay $2 or $3 for a nice pressed-glass cruet with its original stopper. Some of them were plain, but many had patterns—thus the term pattern glass. Eventually, I was scouring antique shows and shops everywhere for new cruets. I would be lucky to find a good new piece at $4 to $6, yet, the stoppers were often long gone. Then my quest expanded to finding complete sets—cruets and their original stoppers.

At a meeting of underwriters in Vancouver, British Columbia, where I was giving a talk on insurance, I mentioned in passing my interest in collecting vinegar cruets. Later, a very distinguished British gentleman came up to me and asked if I knew anything about fine art glass, particularly Galle *(Figure 5)*. Frankly, I didn't. He said to me, "Well, you have an interest in this, let me show you."

My new friend led me to a fine shop in downtown Vancouver. With an easy familiarity, he opened a cabinet and removed an exquisite vinegar cruet that had a scene cut into what seemed like layers of glass. It was like a master painting on glass, and I was sufficiently fascinated to consider paying up to $30 or $40—and then I saw the price—$170.

5 | *Galle vase*

I wish I could say that I bought that Galle cruet on the spot because I am sure that now it would be worth over $2,000. However, the fascination never left me: I went back home to learn how anything could be made that beautifully, not to mention, command such prices. I found a remarkable book on French cameo glass that made me realize I was looking at an art form—one that warranted my devotion. Although I have since expanded that ardor to become an expert on a wide range of collectibles, one's first love is always the most sentimental.

But if you think you can claim sentiment when applying for a loan to launch your collecting venture, just try it. When I think of what I did, it makes me shudder. I borrowed $40,000 against my life insurance renewals to finance a search of the Northwest for fine cameo glass. If you're lucky—and I was—you will find an understanding banker. If not, there are always your relatives.

Speaking of relatives, my wife Jeanie has provided an abiding tolerance for my hobby over the years. In the 1950s when we toured the Northwest to buy every piece of cameo glass we could find, carved glass was more of a curiosity than a valued collectible. The only people who really specialized in cameo were those who knew of it firsthand from travels in France or those few who recognized it as highly collectible. Yet Jeanie was always patient with me in this regard.

I well recall our first acquisition—from a wonderful shop owned by Jenny Welch in the Mount Hood area of Oregon. When I paid $90 for that 6-inch piece of glass signed "Michel," it was easy to see some misgiving (or was it incredulity?) on my wife's face. When she suggested we stop for a hamburger on the way home, I'm not sure she saw the humor when I said, "We can't afford it."

Not only have I had a hard time assuring my family of the underlying soundness of collecting, others have expressed amazement as well—even those known to be antique fanciers themselves. I once ran into columnist Doug Baker at a fine antique show at the Portland Memorial Coliseum. "What have you got, Bob?" he asked. I handed him a rather attractive cameo piece in autumn colors. My eyes darted nervously between the concrete floor of the Coliseum and my relinquished prized possession as I anxiously watched him roll it back and forth in his hands. When I told him that what he held was worth $140, he gripped it considerably tighter and gingerly handed it back to me. "My friend," he said, "that is not a vase. It is a v-a-a-a-se!"

I had lunch with Doug the next day and, with the devil in his eye, he said, "Watch the paper tonight." So I did. There was a fine write-up about antique dealers. I couldn't, however, escape noticing mention of "this antique nut tearing around buying all the cameo glass he could get his hands on." Doug had christened me an "antique nut," and I confess to his accuracy.

Although a certain amount of indulgence, both financial and sentimental, is part of
the game, that indulgence must always be tempered with good judgment — even
when it seems that anything but reason is prevailing.

My friend Doug didn't get a chance to see a piece I had bought previously at that
Coliseum show. I saw it the moment I entered: A striking vase over two and one-
half feet high, set on a late Victorian table which stood in the middle of a large
display area of magnificent furnishings. Its hue went from white to gray, and it had
a motif of birch trees with snow-laden branches. Scattered about the base were
blackbirds. The vase didn't just sit there; nothing that spectacular could. It was
revolving and spotlighted to show off its beauty. I was transfixed as I realized I was
gazing at a choice piece of Daum French Cameo. Its $500 price, however, brought
me quickly back to earth. But even at that price, I knew I'd better not just dream
about it: there were too many other people contemplating it. I flat-out bought it
without quibbling. Later, I discovered the match to this piece at a Chicago gallery.
The price was $5,000 — and that was several years ago. Do my wife and I treasure
that piece? You bet we do. In fact, it's as close to being protected by an armed
security guard as anything we have.

So you see, sometimes collecting is a matter of "he who hesitates is lost." This was
borne out by what the dealer did after I bought that particular vase. He asked if I
would leave it there for a few hours with the sold sign on it. When I came back, he
told me that at least forty people had wanted to purchase the piece once it was

marked sold. Still, the reverse is just as often true: he who doesn't hesitate is lost. If you learn your lessons well, you can have the satisfaction of being enough of an authority to buy wisely.

It is one thing to buy on familiar turf, from a dealer or shop where you feel comfortable. But when traveling, if you are like me, it is a temptation to stop at every shop along the way. During a particular quest for lamps from the Art Deco period and before (preferably bronze, certainly Tiffany and Handel lamps and bases), I was lucky enough to find an antique shop in Fresno that was open on Sunday. When I asked the shop owner if he had any good old lamps, he said, "I have a base you might be interested in." With that, he brought out from the back of the shop a Verdi Gris, green patina bronze, with lily pads on the columnar base and bronze supports extending from the lower pedestal to the fitter top *(Figure 7)*. It had three spider arms, holding a ten-inch circular rim. Even the light-socket fitting and chain were original.

When I turned it over, I was thrilled to see a felt label marked "Handel." I was certain the base plate itself was also stamped "Handel," even though the cloth covered it. I asked the shop owner if he had the matching shade for it, and he said, "No, that's the problem. I've had this base for years and I can't find the shade to match it." He quoted a very fair price for the base, so I paid for it and left with my lucky purchase, sans shade.

It did not take long for my burst of enthusiasm to dissipate, however, when I realized how presumptuous it was for me to think I would find what the shop owner couldn't. Furthermore, I did not want just compatibility, I wanted that perfect match — Handel to Handel. By the time we arrived in Palm Springs, I had sadly reconciled myself to the prospect of searching for years for the particular shade I wanted. Then, we took a sidetrip to Yucca Valley, where we had heard of a wonderful antique shop off the beaten path.

The owner welcomed us warmly, and we sat in her parlorlike atmosphere and talked shop (pardon the pun). My eyes maintained polite contact with hers, while at the same time taking in her fine antiques. A lamp shade, almost hidden on a high shelf, caught my attention despite its mantle of dust. I asked the shop owner if she would bring it down so I could have a look.

As she did, I was astonished to see that it looked as though it might match my recently purchased base. Sure enough, closer inspection bore out my high hopes. The color of the florals in the shade was the exact color of my base, and the rim of the shade was a perfect fit. And when I saw the Handel signature, I couldn't believe my good fortune. As I gaze at it today, I am reminded that serendipity is one of the greatest joys of collecting.

7 | *Verdi Gris bronze*
Handel lamp

AUCTIONS

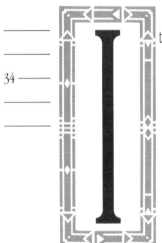 t is my opinion that a good auction house is one of the most satisfactory ways of disposing of those excellent antiques and large estates. Many attorneys and bankers are finding this out as well. The better the reputation of the auction house and the better-known the auctioneer, the more likely it is that they will continue to receive consignment referrals.

Auctions are a tricky business, however; in this chapter I will try to separate the wheat from the chaff. Let's start with a prime example of what an exciting and lucrative event an auction can be—and how valuable it can be to an appraiser to gain all the background knowledge he can before finishing his appraisal for an auction.

Years ago, the Hoyt Hotel in Portland, Oregon, decided to sell its famed Barbary Coast collection. The bank concerned wanted Harvey Dick, the owner and collector of all of these interesting items, to have a say in the selection of the appraiser. They suggested that Harvey might want to talk to me and find out my qualifications for helping dispose of his fascinating and certainly personally treasured items.

A meeting was set up for 2:00 the next day with Harvey. In order to get a little background information, I went to the bar in the Hoyt Hotel and sat musing over a cup of tea and looking at those beautiful hanging shades. One of the greatest sources of information is a bartender, so I casually said to him, "These shades are so beautiful and they all look old—do you know if any of them are new?"

He shrugged and said, "Harvey Dick collected these over many years and the only one that is new is that one right up there." With that, he pointed to a magnificent shade

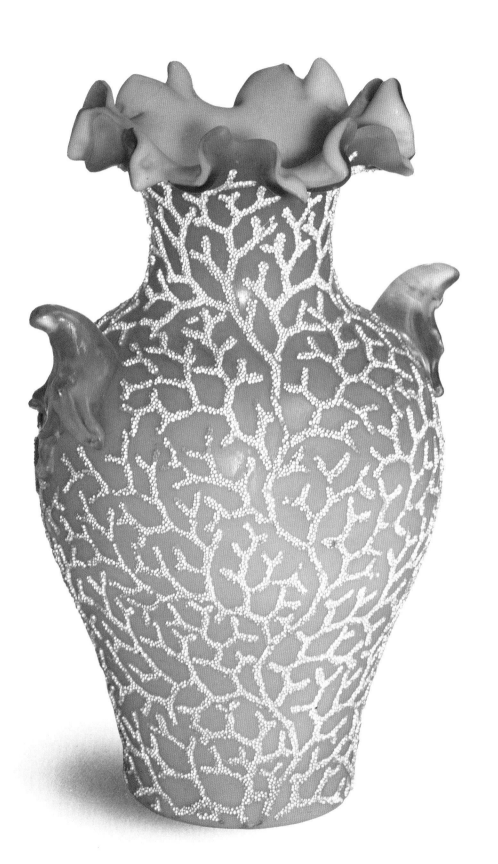

8 | *Coralene vase*

hanging directly over the end of the bar. Well, I thanked him, drank my tea, and left. An hour later, I met Harvey, who looked at me quizzically and said, "Bob, there are some 104 hanging leaded shades in this place; 103 of them are old, and one of them is new. Can you tell me which is the new one?"

Well, I made a rather studied walk around the whole place looking at all of the shades, and when I came back to him I said, "Harvey, they are all just outstanding, but I have my doubts about that one hanging there at the end of the bar."

He looked at me and said, "That's amazing—you've got the job."

I never did tell the bank about that ploy—and maybe it has been partly on my conscience—so now I've confessed.

I had the pleasure of making the presale evaluation and estimate of return for the hotel and the bankers. The initial step was to determine whether to dispose of the collection through auction or by private sale. In my mind, there was no contest as to which approach would yield the highest return. I estimated that approximately $200,000 could be realized in a personal sale; on the other hand, the probable return in a well-handled auction would be between $300,000 and $350,000. So, the owner and creditors decided on an auction.

The Hoyt Hotel was an old structure. From the second floor on up, it was much like any of the full-block-stone transient hotels found in urban centers. But that first floor belied any sense of decay. Within the lobby, dining rooms, and Barbary Coast showrooms, there were 104 table lamps and hanging lamps—in signed Tiffany, signed Handel, and unsigned, leaded shades. Throughout, the massive Victorian furniture was made of oak, walnut, and mahogany. There were four separate bars. One—for men only—was typical of the rough 1890 saloons, with an open grate in front and running water beneath. (When I say rough, I mean rough.) For more refined patrons, there was a highly polished, honey-oak bar, with a back bar housing a large, beveled mirror. The finest bar of all was in the Roaring 20s room, which was the size of a Las Vegas casino showroom. This bar was of black walnut, about sixty feet long, with four huge pillars supporting a back bar with a sectioned, beveled mirror. Just to remind us that we were in the wild west, a distinct bullet hole remained in the right-hand corner.

Off from the Roaring 20s room was the Gay 90s cocktail lounge, fitted with the best in Victorian tables and chairs and extending half the length of the block. The Hoyt Hotel was a showplace that hosted people from all over the country.

The appraisal had to be done at night to prevent word from leaking out about the upcoming sale. So from midnight until 6:00 a.m., for four nights in a row, I wandered through these rooms filled with haunting nostalgia. When I was finished, the bankers and the owner, Harvey Dick, sat down with me and asked, "Could an

A reputable appraiser will not estimate simply to satisfy the customer's desired value for an item. Nor will any good appraiser downgrade an item with the intent to purchase it personally. A certified appraiser is bound by the ethics of the profession to give both an honest and an accurate evaluation.

auction possibly bring half-a-million?" My response was a qualified maybe. I
thought *if* the emotional impact of the event was captured, and *if* it was presented
well, there was a chance of reaching that figure.

More than $10,000 was spent in promotion alone, with full-page ads in the big-
circulation antique publications. The ads were imaginative — and they worked.
Inquiries poured in at an unbelievable rate. People came from all over the country,
and previews extended for over a week. The nostalgia was infectious, and soon
marvelous stories were aired and printed — the type of publicity that couldn't be
bought at any price.

The first night of the auction seemed like a scene straight out of Hollywood. Floodlights
swept the sky. Television interviewers caught celebrities as they entered. Seats were
only $10 per person, so it was an event attended by more than just the privileged.
With seven hundred seats sold, promotion costs were practically recouped, and the
auction had yet to begin.

The expectant atmosphere pulsated with people, music, and exhilaration. As the
auctioneer strode to center stage, he was resplendent in white tie and tails. Two
attendants carried a shade to the customized black display box. The houselights
dimmed, and a hidden spotlight revealed a gleaming leaded hanging shade. The
seven hundred gasps in response proved the effectiveness of the setting.

As the eager buyers leaned forward and the urge to bid began, I knew what was going
to happen. That first unsigned shade, *(Figure 6)* which I had appraised at $900,

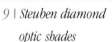

9 | *Steuben diamond*
optic shades

*10 \ Steuben blue
Aurene bowl*

sold for $1,900. The pattern was set. Forty shades—including a number of fine Steuben shades *(Figure 9)*—were sold that night at prices ranging from 100 to 200 percent higher than the original appraisal. Those sales made history: the value of fine leaded and individual glass shades soon went up all over the country.

This was no gimmick; it was no shilling. It was a veritable stage production that moved people to buy. The Hoyt auction, showing how it works when it works best, was an example of great planning and great delivery. For that kind of delivery, you need a consummate auctioneer.

The good auctioneer needs to have background knowledge and be aware of its approximate value. As was done at the Hoyt auction, fine items should be displayed dramatically, so they are promoted for maximum effect.

However, not all auctions are run so effectively. Some auction houses work on a volume basis—so many items per minute. It doesn't seem to matter to them if it is a Dresden figurine or a made-in-occupied-Japan ashtray. To me, this lack of interest seems unfair for the exceptional item.

In other cases, apathy is due to lack of knowledge. I have seen uninformed auctioneers hold up a piece of pressed glass and ask, "What am I offered for this piece of glass?" They may then recite the same litany for a piece of Tiffany. This indifference is great for the educated buyer, but sad for the seller.

The auctioneer's knowledge and abilities are not the only factors to take into account. Sometimes, what the bidders don't know *can* hurt. A friend of mine once popped in at an auction, where she saw a hanging light fixture, circa 1920. She bid on it and got it at a fair price. Unbeknownst to her, however, that bid was per-shade for a lot of forty. She was saved only because the shades were white translucent. A gifted china painter, she simply decorated and sold the extras, actually profiting by her mistake. You might not be so lucky, though—and most auction houses insist that lot purchases be honored.

It also helps to be aware of experienced bidders who try to dominate an auction. Some are so intimidating that their reputation precedes them. Let's go back to the Hoyt Hotel to learn how one person beat such a bidder at his own game. Remember the bar with the bullet hole in the mirror? When the time came for it to be auctioned, a gentleman from San Francisco—well-known in these parts as intransigent—sat on the edge of the bar and held his bidding card high. He was literally staking claim. Another gentleman, an acquaintance of mine from Montana, also wanted that bar very badly. Here's what happened.

The bidding began, and soon it was just the two of them, rather quietly upping the ante. At $10,000, Mr. Montana threw in the towel. In the full flush of victory, Mr. San Francisco toasted to his own success. Then quite a turnabout occurred.

11 \ Queen Anne
   chest reproduction

Earlier that day, it just so happened that Mr. Montana had calculated the odds of his wresting the bar from his formidable opponent. So he had a cashier's check drawn, made payable to Mr. San Francisco. When he stopped his bidding that evening, it was with that card up his sleeve.

Mr. Montana came over with a glass of scotch, handed it to Mr. San Francisco, and held aloft the cashier's check made out for $15,000. "How would you like to make $5,000 in about two minutes. I will take the bar off your hands and save you the expense of moving it. Besides that, I'll throw in this glass of scotch and we can toast the Hoyt Hotel. What do you say?"

Mr. San Francisco looked from the scotch to the check, then back to the man from Montana. "You've got a deal," he said.

Sure, he got a quick $5,000 profit. But Mr. Montana got the bar he wanted, at less than he might have paid with continual bidding. It was one of the cleverest coups I've ever seen in bidding—discrete, yet direct.

To be sure, less-than-discrete and less-than-honest bidding does go on. Occasionally, buyers will collude if there are several of the same item. I saw this happen at one auction, where there were forty-five great pieces of cut glass. I overheard several buyers plan their strategy this way: "John, you can have the first two, and I won't bid against you. Then I'll take the next two," etc. This went on to the extent that signed, 9-inch, well-cut Libby and Fry bowls went for as little as $60 and $65. This was certainly unfortunate for the consignor.

Now this could not happen in a large sale where there are hundreds of buyers, nor would it happen in a specialty sale. No few individuals can corner the market at a well-publicized auction held for items of great value.

However, other bidders are not the only ones you have to beware of at an auction. Sometimes it's yourself you have to watch out for. A word to the wise is: attend an auction determined to bid only with reason, rather than emotion—unless you can well afford your emotion. For an example, let's return once more to the Hoyt Hotel.

At one point, a heavy-leaded fountain lamp, about four-feet high and on a bronze base, was put up for auction. I knew someone who was willing to go up to $800 for that piece. Bidding was rising at a pace of $100 per offer, and quickly passed $800. I thought to myself, "That's too bad. My friend won't get his lamp."

Without looking back, I heard a persistent bidder literally shouting from sheer excitement. When the loud bidder was victorious at $2,600, I turned around to see who this tenacious winner was. I stared in disbelief at my friend who was holding his bidding card up, with a glazed look in his eyes. He exclaimed, "Bob, what in the world have I done?" I had no answer for him, but I wasn't too concerned because I knew he was in a position to afford his emotional bid.

It is not unheard of for decoys to be placed in auctions, people who pose as bidders only to force the price up. The slang term shilling, *usually reserved for confidence schemes, also applies here. Some brave souls, if they suspect a shilling, will confront the house on it. If you are mistaken, all you have to lose is your pride.*

At the end of that four-day auction, sales totaled over half-a-million dollars. Of course, its success could not be attributed solely to chance. Of all the events of its kind that I have attended, the Hoyt auction was the best-organized and best-managed. That is no small feat, considering how emotional auctions can be.

At another auction, one of my pieces provoked an unusual display. It was the top casing of a signal light that I had made into a bell with a cut-glass prism handle, a silver chain, and glass striker bead. Although it was attractive, it was actually quite a mishmash. I thought it might bring $30 at auction, so was utterly amazed when bidding reached $75.

Then I heard an avid bidder state, "I used to own that bell, and now I'm going to get it back." The attractive ladies he was with seemed impressed with his determination, especially when it cost him $140. Not wanting to interfere with his capturing the bell (and the belles), I didn't tell him it was impossible for him to have ever owned that makeshift bell.

If you feel confident about your self-control, then all you really need to know in order to succeed at auction bidding are some fundamentals to which any legitimate house will adhere. First of all, if the auctioneer does not specify in advance of the bidding what the house rules are, ask—or examine the catalog.

One thing you should discover is whether items are reserved. A reserve is just that: a reservation to sell or not to sell. This may be determined by the consignor, who wants to prevent the item from selling at a ridiculously low price. Without a reserve, his or her only recourse would be to buy it back and pay the auction commission. On the other hand, sometimes, a reserve is determined by the house when selling house items. If there are reserves, usually the house gives a written statement to the consignor to the effect that the reserve figure has been accepted and that the item will not be sold for less.

A bidder might have no apparent competition and wonder why his or her bid is not accepted. In this event, the auctioneer might explain directly that the bid is below the reserve.

Or perhaps someone is bidding on behalf of the owner in an attempt to reach the reserve. Most auctioneers don't allow the owner to bid on his or her own item; but frankly, the owner may be unknown or have a proxy. While this is not ethical on the owner's part, even an honest and reputable house cannot always prevent it.

Most houses charge for items that do not reach the reserve, as well as those that do. Whether this 5 to 10 percent is openly listed as a buy-back charge, or is hidden in storage, handling, or insurance costs, there will surely be some costs involved in selling your items at auction.

Consignment costs should always be indicated on the receipts. It is just common sense never to leave anything with anybody without a receipt and a clear understanding of the process and charges involved. No legitimate house would object to having everything in writing.

Finally, buying without preview is foolish and expensive. Always inspect items carefully in advance because it is a commonplace policy with auctions to allow no recourse after the fact. This caveat is usually stipulated somewhere, either in the catalog or verbally in advance of the bidding.

I've talked about the conduct of auctions, but have said very little regarding whether they are a good place to buy. You can bet they are! Sure, there will be distinctive items so desired that spirited bidding may force them out of your reach. But I have been to auctions, and perhaps you have too, where there is only one person who wants a particular item—and gets it at a good price. If that person happens to be you, all the better. Yet even when there is a contest and the bidding gets brisk, that may be your only chance to get the item of your dreams. Then, only you can determine what is a "reasonable" price. Since the desirability and beauty of a collectible is in the "eye of the beholder," the price you can afford and are willing to pay *is* your reasonable price.

Auction houses of excellent repute will more than meet the requirements needed to protect their good names. These houses also employ a staff of experts available for buyers to consult for selective choices. So, armed with your new knowledge, let the bidding begin.

ESTATE SALES

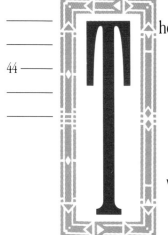

The term "estate sale" is sometimes a misnomer—for instance, when referring to other liquidation sales, such as moving or conservator sales. For the sake of brevity, I will restrict myself to what makes up a professionally handled estate sale, with the understanding that some people use the term loosely. One need only look at the classified section of any newspaper to see how many people are getting into the act. Therefore, it is imperative that professionals be just that if they don't want to fall by the wayside.

Why is it a good idea to put your possessions in the hands of qualified estate sales people? First of all, their regular followers will come to your sale. Secondly, you are guaranteed good promotion, knowledge of the value of your items, optimum liquidation, and a return of 70 to 75 percent of the designated value.

Just to give you an example of the importance of an estate sale being handled professionally, let me tell what happened once when I noticed a homespun version some time ago. Naturally, when I saw the sign, "Estate Sale," my car braked by itself, without my even realizing it. As I walked toward the house, the owner met me and, to my delight, said, "Aren't you Mr. Rau? Can you help me with a piece of glass I am wondering about?" I told her I'd be glad to.

I was then stunned to see a fine agata tumbler being passed along casually. Agata is a very rare form of art glass, shaded somewhere from pink to tan to mauve, with bluish splotches that look almost like an abstract ink-spot design. For the art-glass devotee, it is much sought after. I asked the owner, "Do you realize this is a piece of

13 | *Period tea safe*

agata, worth between $400 and $600?" The dear lady turned pale and said, "Hold this a minute." She ran back inside her house and returned with yet another, with the children's toothbrushes still in it. How it survived two brushings a day (maybe only one if the kids had their way) without being chipped or cracked, is beyond me. When we washed off the toothpaste, we could recognize a fine agata tumbler.

After she handed me the second one, she tore off her apron, pulled on her coat, and flew out the door, telling me she'd be back in twenty minutes. There I stood with two precious tumblers, not wanting to set them down, but not sure what the story was or just what I should do. So I carried them around with me until she returned.

Her triumphant return heralded yet two more of the rare tumblers. "Now we have them all," she exclaimed.

"Where in the world did these last two come from?" I asked.

"I gave these to the kids yesterday to take to the school rummage sale. I found them priced at 50 cents each."

Luckily, she was able to retrieve them before the rummage sale began. There are enough discerning collectors around who would have grabbed them—and then probably fainted. The moral of the story is: Get help from professionals when pricing items you are ready to part with.

There are people who will help you price things for a small percentage, and then you handle your own sale. You may have to rely on word-of-mouth to find such a person: Unfortunately, they seldom advertise; maybe now they will. This is not a bad way to go if you are willing to handle the other problems inherent in a liquidation sale of any kind.

Let's say, however, that you have decided to make it a formal estate sale. There are some dos and don'ts about finding the best seller.

Start by attending various sales conducted by different people. Observe their approach toward the sale. How do they mark the items? What kind of help do they hire? How are buyers treated? Since you will be trusting your prized possessions to them, it is important to find a good match.

Once you feel comfortable with your instinctive choice, back it up with concrete referrals from several individuals who have used that seller. Ask to see letters of reference if you don't know any of their previous clients.

Determine what type of advertising is used and whether you pay separately for it or if it is included as a part of the service.

Evaluate how effective the promotion is from the perspective of street traffic. It is easy to give proper directions to a sale located in the middle of town on easy-access streets, but it can be a real work of art to get buyers into outlying areas. If you live on the outskirts, make sure the seller knows how to get buyers there—and then does it.

Get a presale evaluation. If you have antiques, make sure the evaluation is done by a qualified appraiser. It is wise to discuss the purpose of the evaluation with your appraiser to determine the potential market value of your estate or moving sale. Once aware of this, the appraiser should abide by the tenet outlined in the chapter entitled "Appraisals"—that is, to appraise an item accurately with no attempt to ingratiate himself with the owner by giving excessive values.

Regardless of the accuracy or professionalism of the evaluation, you have no recourse if the net result is less than anticipated. There are many factors beyond your control. If the big game of the season goes into extra innings or the weather turns bad and the game is cancelled, your ballpark figure will be affected as well.

After you have decided to commit your items to sale is not the time to get sentimental. If you pull a $100 item out of the sale, it could cost the seller up to $25 in commission. If he or she has spent five hours setting up a display of your costume jewelry and then you take back the better pieces, you will reap frustration and resentment—and perhaps even a less-satisfactory job by the seller.

15 | Staffordshire box

Once you decide to trust your seller, do just that. Give him or her the authority and
control to do the job. I know of one case where the owner, a recent widower, placed
his sale in the hands of a top professional. Then, the day before the sale, this kindly
man let his neighbor take every piece of cut glass that was signed Fry, Hawkes, and
Libby—for the sake of "remembrance." Unforgivably, the neighbor exploited the
poor widower, walking out with more than $1,000 in the best cut glass. It was later
discovered that she actually sold the pieces. If you decide to have an estate sale,
consult your seller before you bend the rules.

Along the same line of letting the pro do it for you, don't hover too much during the
pricing and displaying of your items. Your emotions are bound to get in the way.
While your great-grandmother's pressed glass bowl may have a great deal of
sentimental value to you, your seller knows its true market value. He or she should
not set prices based on subjective value unless it is realistic to do so. You must
remember that even though you own the items you have turned them over to
someone else to sell. Your interference can be costly, both in time and dollars.

Many people now handling estate sales take an extra precaution to prevent misunder-
standings, one I believe to be very wise: They draw up an agreement to be signed by
both parties. Then if a problem should come up, the agreement also details the
process both parties have agreed on to resolve any differences. Even though a hand
shake would suffice in most cases, it never hurts to have everything in writing. Most
estate sales professionals have a form that is clearly understood and can be easily
and quickly completed.

So now that you know how to properly conduct an estate sale—by letting the proper
people do it—let's talk about what to do if you are the one wanting to buy.

As I mentioned at the beginning of the chapter, the classified section of the newspaper
is full of ads for estate sales. If one interests you, see if it specifies that numbers will
be handed out for admission in sequence. If numbers are given out, it is an
indication that it will be a good sale. You can expect that, if there is a time specified
for handing out numbers, they will not be given out a minute before that specified
time, but people will start lining up hours in advance. It used to be that you had to
wait for hours to get your number, only to return hours later to stand in line again
for the actual opening of the sale. Now, however, some enterprising souls have
streamlined the process a bit. As you arrive, you secure a number and a time to
return—sort of like a dinner reservation.

If you want to attend a sale that has drawn a huge turnout and you end up with a high
admittance number, don't get discouraged. If the sale is good with thousands of
items available, it is not likely that the first forty people will walk out with the lion's
share. Some people just want to pick up that piece of rose medallion, or the cane

*Unfortunately, some people
enter the business of con-
ducting estate sales just to
make a quick profit—often
at the expense of the owner.
Probably the worst behavior
known is actual embezzle-
ment. This can take the form
of appropriating the better
items for personal profit.
Sometimes the seller enters
into collusion with an outside buyer. In these cases, the
seller may exploit the fact
that sales are slow (which is
largely the seller's own
doing) and call in the buyer,
who promises to buy up what
is left.*

chair, that was advertised. You might find—on the last day—a particularly choice piece of Steuben that was not advertised and that everyone else passed by because of the price tag. *(Figure 10)*

A sale's attendance is an excellent way to determine its quality (if you are interested in buying) and the capability of the seller (if you are interested in hiring). Watch the ads for time and place, then drive by to see if the turnout is significant. An extremely effective sale can bring people out by the hundreds.

I'll never forget the time I found an estate sale on its third day. Not much was left— except for one rather interesting item. It was a small, footed cup in pressed glass with a $12 price tag. I couldn't believe it was still there. You see, it was pink slag in the princess feather pattern, with great coloring and in remarkable condition. How this had survived the onslaught of scrutinizing buyers is beyond me. It was easily worth $300, so I am convinced that "sleepers" do exist. Personally, I also think it is great fun to go to a sale during the last three hours, when prices are reduced considerably and bidding (both verbal and written) is open.

Another idea is to call the seller to see if what you want is available. If so, try asking the person handing out numbers just where in the house your choice items might be. They may tell you, they may not—it never hurts to ask. I saw someone once dash downstairs and pick off about thirty great items—while everyone else flocked on the main floor—solely because he had found out in advance what was being sold and where it was.

But even if you are not privy to such information, remember that the placement of items can be strategic from the seller's viewpoint. Good sellers won't ignore a system that works for them—and that system may be to place teasers in odd places to get people to really scour.

While sellers encourage scouring, hoarding without an honest intent to buy is highly discouraged. Many sellers now will not permit people to pick up items that strike their fancy, only to weed through it all at the checkout. You had better be prepared to buy whatever you put in your box. You must also be prepared to pay full price at most professionally run estate sales, at least on the first day.

Often, major items not sold on the first day for full price will be available at reduced cost on the second or third day. While some sellers have a fixed reduction and are usually consistent about the amount, there is great variance on these reductions between sellers. So it helps to know your seller and learn his or her habits. For example, one seller might reduce any items priced at $20 or less by 50 percent, and items priced at more than $20 by 25 percent. Another seller might work solely on an offer basis. If you are good at dickering, this may suit you perfectly. To me, it's the hard way; but if you enjoy the game, more power to you.

16 | *Wicker portrait chair*

Of course, throughout an estate sale, offers can be submitted in writing on a bid basis. This is a very straightforward approach. You simply note the time, the article, the amount you are willing to pay, your name, and phone number. Then you hope your bid is accepted as the best offer.

As to the amount to bid, it is sometimes hard to tell. Let's assume an upright phonograph is marked $160, and you don't want to go that high. I suggest making an irregular bid, such as $130.10. It just might surpass other bids because of the irregular amount. However, don't split hairs. Remember, if you really want something and you hold out for a few dollars less, you might lose it altogether.

Be prepared to honor a written bid. It is not fair to the seller if you affect a sale by a written bid and then change your mind. If you do that, some estate sellers will not hesitate to make their feelings clear to you—in no uncertain terms. It is just not worth the embarrassment.

It all comes down to using your best judgment and discretion when making an open offer. Making an offer or bid is a game, but a game that has rules to be observed if you want to play. The individual who stands in the middle of the room and blatantly says, "I'll give you $125 for this thing," usually doesn't get too far.

So now you have your choice item. What recourse is available to you if it turns out to be damaged? Unfortunately, not much. You might bring it to the seller and explain the situation. But most likely you will be told that prices are based on as-is conditions. Considering how heavily items are handled in an estate sale, a fleck off a piece of porcelain is not really grounds for a refund.

It is not misrepresentation if an item is sold as-is and the buyer just didn't realize it— although he or she probably should have. Yet, gross misrepresentation does occur sometimes. The example that comes to my mind was not at a professional estate sale, but at a similar type of house sale.

A couple expressed an interest in art glass to an individual having a house sale. He then took them upstairs and opened up a trunk, which contained several pieces of "Coralene" wrapped in newspaper dated 1918. Coralene *(Figure 8)* is a glass that has delicate and intricate beading over a quality Victorian surface. It is a fine process. When it is authentic, with the beads solidly affixed and kiln treated, it is rare and very valuable. The seller told the couple, "These have been up here since my grandmother died." I can well imagine their excitement as they watched the unfolding of what they thought was exquisitely rare art glass from 1918 newspaper.

The couple proudly brought their seven newly acquired, beautiful pieces of "Coralene" to me for evaluation. However, although lovely, the pieces shown to me were not authentic. They were some fairly good pieces of satin glass with cheap beads glued on in a pattern. The beads even came off if you pushed at them with a fingernail.

Just imagine the seller purposely wrapping that glass in old newspaper, putting it in the old trunk, and practicing his line until an unsuspecting buyer came along.

Almost anyone could be fooled by such a stage setting. I suppose the only safe way is: Never buy if there is any doubt about the circumstances. If it seems too good to be true, it probably is.

On a lighter note, I once heard a wonderful story where everyone involved was fooled, but there was no villain. In the East, a furniture manufacturer who specializes in reproductions of the greatest pieces of Queen Anne, Hepplewhite, and Sheraton bought an original Queen Anne chest, *(Figure 11)* then reproduced it, even down to the perfume spot inside the drawer, and blown-in dust—which was sprayed in from a can (this is really available). The manufacturer properly represented the piece as a reproduction when it was first sold. However, when items are resold a few times, things can get confusing.

A different furniture manufacturer also wanted to make quality reproductions and scoured the country for originals. By great fortune, this manufacturer's representative heard of a magnificent Queen Anne chest, owned by a gentleman in Kansas. He paid the very reasonable figure of $3,000.00 for an original and shipped it back to his employer. To everyone's dismay, when it was displayed in all of its magnificence, one of the artisans exclaimed, "That is the one I made two years ago when I was working for the company back East!"

So, it can happen to the best of us. Take heart, though, and keep in mind that estate sales in all their current forms can be a delightful experience. They don't have to be big sales, and they don't necessarily have to be professionally handled. They just have to be approached with care and common courtesy.

BUYING FROM AN ANTIQUE SHOP

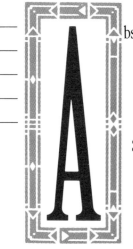

Absolutely the safest way to get the genuine article is through an antique dealer—
assuming that the dealer is honest and responsible, that all the merchandise is
warranted and certified, and that the prices are at fair market value. That assumption is not too unrealistic, because marginal dealers usually don't stay in business
for long.

So if the deliberate approach suits you best, buying from an antique shop is the way to
go. This will not be the bargain hunting of estate sales nor the clamor of an
auction. It will be more methodical, but you can often find the exact item you
want. Whether you seek an old balance scale, *(Figure 12)* a period tea safe,
(Figure 13) or the finest of glass and porcelain, there are dealers whose specialty
will meet your need.

As in any specialty, it is not feasible for an antique dealer to have complete knowledge
of all items. Some shops have a little bit of everything, but most dealers have found
that they do better in their specialty areas than they would with a conglomerate
show-like approach.

The easiest sources for finding the dealers you want are the newspaper and the Yellow
Pages. Most display ads will indicate the type of antiques available. A phone call
can save you a visit—although a visit can be a lot more fun. If you do decide to
visit, it helps to know some protocol.

If you actually just want to browse, fine—but if you really want to be helped, ask. You
are not going to be hassled or harassed to buy. A dealer generally will simply try to

18 | *Reclining Victorian chair, working condition*

help you find what you want. Despite a careful perusal, I have often missed things that were later pointed out by the dealer. One of my most treasured pieces, a sealing-wax-red Lalique bowl, *(Figure 14)* was out of view. The dealer was just waiting for the right collector to come along; when she withdrew it from its secret place beneath her desk, I was so glad I had asked.

There are other aspects of protocol that are more relevant in the large antique shows which are more loosely structured. Although I will discuss those in the next chapter, they also apply to individual shops.

Not only is it likely that a dealer may be harboring a treasured item for you, he or she will also be a font of information about its authenticity. Still, dealers are human, and mistakes can be made. In most cases, however, there is some leniency about returns if a piece is found to be unauthentic.

When you are planning a major purchase, it is best to take along someone who can verify authenticity. Some dealers don't like this, but it can be done subtly. Whoever is doing the evaluating for you can just quietly look the piece over, reserving an opinion for later when the two of you can discuss it in private.

With any piece of transparent or translucent glass, a crack or break is always apparent because of the refraction of light. It may be mended properly; it may be ground down; it may even ding if you flick it—but when held up to light, the repair will show.

If you are a knowledgeable collector, you will know something about assessment yourself. Yet, even so, some of the best collectors have purchased a beautifully decorated gold-lustre Tiffany, only to discover later that it had been cut down and repolished. When the work is well done, it is easy to overlook an interior crack in a restored porcelain. If you take along a friend as discerning as you are, that extra pair of eyes can really help.

Although certain flaws are not terribly detrimental, a damaged item should not be represented at full value. The state-of-the-art in porcelain repair is highly sophisticated; however, once a piece has been repaired or restored, technically it is not the original and should not be represented as such. Conversely, because of what is possible with porcelain repair, I don't hesitate to secure an object, such as a Staffordshire piece, that needs slight repair *(Figure 15).*

Once you decide to buy from an antique shop, you may have several payment options. Unlike estate sales or other liquidation sales where it is cash-and-carry, an antique dealer will generally take credit cards, checks, or even set up a payment plan. Many people prefer the convenience, as well as the better guarantees, of a private shop. So, although sometimes costs are higher, this is offset by great selections, convenience, and peace of mind.

In recent years, dealers have banded together to form antique malls—and the idea is fantastic. Considering that this cooperative approach is an innovative and effective way to cut overhead costs—such as salaries, insurance, and rent—it is no wonder that malls have become so popular. In almost every city or even small

town, you will find these centralized shopping areas advertised in local publications. You may wonder, "Don't the dealers suffer from increased competition?" While that is a fair assumption, it is not the case. Most dealers benefit from being part of a mall that attracts many more shoppers than an isolated shop would find possible. They also have lower rent and advertising costs, and they don't have to put in the long hours traditionally needed to tend shop.

These antique malls operate on a revolving-duty roster, with a handful of people representing all the dealers. How wonderful to be involved only four or five days a month, rather than thirty! Although there are some things on display, most things are locked in cabinets, so it is not high-risk in terms of security. Each dealer gives a small percentage of his or her returns to the owner of the mall. Again, in proportion, the investment is much smaller than a full-shop operation.

The drawbacks to antique malls are that the stock is limited by the amount of space and the mall is often run by people not directly affiliated with your business. While independent antique and collectible shops are still the bulwark of this business, providing collectors with the opportunity to visit regularly and learn continually, the antique malls offer yet another option to collectors. But it is something else again when the dealers set up for show purposes.

IT'S SHOW TIME!

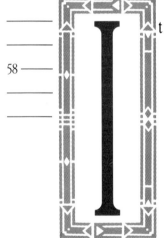t is loads of fun to go to antique shows and see the best of everything. Although perhaps you could see the same items in the dealers' shops, they are seldom as well displayed as in an antique show. It can be mind-boggling (and sometimes a little intimidating) to walk in to an antique show and see a $60,000 Tiffany lamp on the first table.

Shows alone seldom provide a living for most dealers. Overhead is significant when preparing for a show. There is the high cost of booths; costly insurance for transporting items; the expense of displaying, merchandising, and marketing; not to mention the hard work of packing and unpacking. However, the show itself is not the end result of all this effort. The dealers are building reputations and laying the groundwork for future sales back at the shop.

Of course, this assumes that the dealer is native to the area. Many fine dealers from other areas bring remarkable things that are not typical to the host region. What a pleasure it is to see what is being shown in other parts of the country — and what an opportunity to buy exotic items! But whether the show is with local dealers or those from somewhere else, all will agree that the first two hours of a show are crucial to the sales. Primary interest is aroused at the beginning of a show, when buyers are alert.

As a consequence, the first rule of protocol I will mention with regard to these large, loosely structured shows is: Take pity on the poor harried dealer who is trying to develop as much of that potential as possible. This is not the time or place for shop

20 \ *Period magazine rack*

talk, unless it is about an item you want to buy. Maybe they would love to discuss the piece that Aunt Nellie had that is so similar to theirs—later—but probably not early on.

Perhaps belonging at the top of the list of show protocol is how (and whether) to handle the merchandise. Keep in mind that the fine antique furniture is not there for your comfort and convenience. One should never rest on a chair arm, lounge on a davenport, or bounce on a wicker portrait chair *(Figure 16)* to test its firmness. If you simply want to rest, most shows provide rest areas as an accommodation for weary shoppers.

As for picking up breakable items, do so at your own risk. It is reasonable to want to examine crystal, porcelain, silver, etc. Yet I sometimes think there should be a course taught in the proper way to handle these fine items. I so well recall one man who turned over a Tiffany zodiac inkwell to look for the Tiffany Studios signature. The only problem was that he did not realize the original glass liner in blue lustre was still inside. When he turned it over, the top came unhinged and out fell a $200 error in judgment.

It is a difficult situation, and dealers have various thoughts about allowing customers to handle merchandise. If you see a sign that says, "Don't Touch," the message is clear. If you don't feel comfortable about handling precious items, ask the dealer for help.

Remember that most items are priced according to what the dealer thinks is reasonable. If you think a price is too high, ask if the dealer will take less. Just be prepared to take "no" for an answer.

Finally, although most dealers acknowledge the depth of knowledge many individual collectors have, a show is not the place to claim superior knowledge. Occasionally, it is true that a collector may recognize a piece that is incorrectly labeled or evaluated. If that information is conveyed quietly at a time convenient to the dealer, it will probably be welcome. It will not be welcome if it in any way embarrasses or harasses the dealer. Remember, the collector has the distinct advantage of specialized knowledge, whereas the dealer has a broader expertise without the benefit of such specialization.

In order to appeal to a greater market, many dealers are now taking their shows to the shopping malls. These "mall shows" involve simply displaying wares on tables strewn the length of the mall. Although this is not particularly the place to find those fine antiques you may be looking for, it is an excellent source for other items of a collectible nature. These mall shows run the gamut of popular items—from oak and white-pine furniture to the various types of collectible glass—for both the avid and the casual collector.

Although shoplifting is not a funny subject, I cannot resist sharing one memorable
 attempt during one of these mall shows. A man was actually bold enough to grab a
 large and expensive lace tablecloth, step behind an oak cabinet, and quickly wrap
 the cloth underneath his coat. As he strolled out, a dealer noticed that the fellow's
 slip was showing. Since he did not look like the type of guy to wear a lace petticoat,
 he was apprehended and later jailed.

All in all, these dealers have their hands full at a show. They should be congratulated
 for continuing to find ways to provide great items and excellent service.

FLEA MARKETS

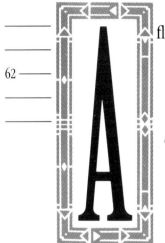

A flea market can certainly be fun when it comes to bantering and bartering. It is a place where unlicensed, small-profit collectors actually make a living by selling not only from their own collections but also what they bought the week before. It is also the place where novices can sell their odds and ends. Most major metropolitan areas have flea markets every weekend.

To assure a space for selling, you should reserve the tables you want a week or two in advance of the flea market. A phone call may suffice; however, those who are in charge of the flea markets may be leery of reserving space on the strength of a phone call alone. So, sometimes, you must sign an agreement. The day of the market, you simply drive to your tables, unload, and then drive back out to park.

I seldom miss a flea market, but I realized long ago that the general public has a very limited chance to get the real bargains. The sellers are there to buy as well as sell, and they have the double advantage both of being pros and being there first. However, many of the larger shows now have an opening special, or presale. For about $20, you can gain admission to the show the night prior to the opening for the general public. Officially, this presale admission is supposed to be for dealers only—but don't let that stop you. They are willing to take your $20, with or without dealer credentials. It is well worth the slightly steep price, because it will give you the chance to really hunt for those bargains. Incidentally, you won't find this arrangement advertised or promoted in any special way. It is known only by word-of-mouth. In this case, I'm the mouth—so now you know.

If you can't or don't want to go to the presale, you still may get what you are looking for (as well as the unexpected lucky find) during general admission. I have found everything from bolts for a bench vise to a lamp finial, from a Barye Bronze *(Figure 17)* to a set of Hopalong Cassidy collectibles *(Figure 19)*. While great buys may be few and far between, they are there.

As to haggling over price, that is the name of the game. Although many sellers may reject an offer early on, you can take a chance and wait it out. Of course, you risk losing your opportunity completely. I remember one guest on our show who said he has never regretted what he has bought—only what he has passed up. It is always a judgment call.

I have yet to figure out how flea markets are profitable to the seller. I see many of the same sellers, with much the same stock, week after week. I never see them at estate sales, which is only logical since the estate sales and flea markets are both held on weekends. Where the wares sold in flea markets are scrounged up from is beyond me, but apparently, there is no shortage of things to sell. Profitable or not, the sellers seem to be having fun.

I am less mystified about how profitable flea markets are to those who run them. Flea markets flourish all over the nation; some of the really big ones cover, literally, acres of land. As many as a thousand sellers reserve tables at varying costs for three to four days in a row, several times a year. And thousands of people pay three to four dollars each to get in. It is easy to see how the profit is made for those who run the flea markets.

Some flea markets are run for charity. Although many of these are operated as astutely as any Fortune 500 company, others sometimes need help, particularly with regard to pricing. I remember one in particular that was a white-elephant-style sale for a library benefit. I was walking by a panel with several prints hanging on it, priced anywhere from a dime to five dollars. The one that caught my eye was a picture of a Victorian lady framed in a three-inch oval gold Gesso frame that was quite beat-up. At fifteen cents, I couldn't resist buying it. After all, at that price, I certainly didn't have much to lose.

When I got home, I took out my loupe for a closer look. Guess what? It was not a cheap print. It was an original, signed miniature, probably French, and worth quite a bit. I honestly felt like a thief for paying only fifteen cents, so I wrote out a check as a donation to the library to assuage my conscience.

I will say it again: Always get assistance with pricing. If it is for a charitable cause, usually there are many competent people who will provide the appraisal service gratis. Once the pricing is taken care of, there is no place like a flea market if you are itching to bargain.

Uninitiated sellers at a flea market may find themselves sold out before the public even gains entrance. This is not as good as it sounds. The sharp-eyed sellers around you may better recognize the value of your items. If they are eager to take them off your hands, it may be so they can resell them at their own tables—but at much higher prices. Know the value of your items before you sell them.

PUBLICATIONS FOR COLLECTORS

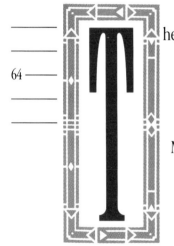

There are many fine publications available on the various aspects of antiques and collectibles. I am continually impressed by the well-written, informative articles that appear in these publications. What an absolutely remarkable job they do in educating people regarding the history and development of certain items. As a result, the public's interest is kept at peak level.

Most of these publications are based on advertising—sellers principally, but also buyers indicating their wants. Most collectors avidly peruse these weekly or monthly publications, searching for specific items which are clearly categorized (i.e., "china," "glass," "furniture," "porcelains," "clocks," etc.) You can go right to the classifieds and see what is available. Then, if you have the spirit of adventure, make a purchase.

It is interesting that many publications allow sellers to advertise items without indicating a price. Truthfully, I wish they would not do that because I don't like ordering blind. It is so much easier to be able to determine whether the price suits the nature of the item, not to mention whether it is in your range.

Typically, the ads are clear-cut. Of all the purchases I have made over the past fifteen years, only once did I receive an item that was not what it was purported to be in the ad. Even that was not a total loss because the seller took the item back. I feel easier buying from recognizable names, those that give a money-back guarantee if the item is returned within five days. Should they not honor a stated return policy, I know the major publications would not continue to accept their ads.

22 | *Victorian tapestry rocker*

As to the buying procedure, it is quite uniform. The buyer sends the seller the money, usually including postage and insurance, and the seller sends the item to the buyer. Don't expect to pay C.O.D. It doesn't work that way. You must be willing to place some trust in the seller. If the item arrives damaged, the claim is placed through the seller, and then the buyer is refunded. If a buyer decides to return an item, he or she also pays the return postage.

Any problems a buyer has with a seller should be reported to the publisher that carried the ad. If there are several complaints, the publisher will probably look into it. One complaint by itself may not be sufficient cause for investigation. A reputable publisher, however, will not continue to accept ads that misinform or misrepresent.

I know of one person whose ads stopped appearing after a while. Before he was caught, he pulled a fast one on me, the post office, and probably several others. I had ordered an 11-inch, signed Handel shade for a signed Harp base I already owned. When it arrived, I suspected something was amiss when I heard the clink of shattered glass in the box. Interestingly enough, when I took it down to the post office for opening, we noticed that the 11-inch shade was packed into a 10-inch box. Obviously, the shade had to have been broken before packing or it would never have fit in the box. Although it was clearly fraud in its intent, the postal authorities are obligated to redeem a claim once they have approved the insurance. So the seller collected on the insurance, and I got a refund. It was technically legal, though certainly unsavory.

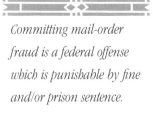

Committing mail-order fraud is a federal offense which is punishable by fine and/or prison sentence.

To further enhance your collecting savvy, subscriptions are available for price guides and price lists. Sometimes people get confused about the difference between a price guide and a price list. The price guide is intended to show a consensus of probable value. It does not break down prices according to region, nor does it take into account wide fluctuations. It is meant to convey an overall impression of value.

Price *lists,* as opposed to price guides, intend to show value based on current asking, selling, and buying prices. The reader can be confused by the extreme disparities between the two. For example, in the price list, you may see that a sulphide marble *(Figure 21)* sold for $20—an extremely low figure. This merely indicates that, at one particular sale, a sulphide marble sold at that price. Price lists and price guides are helpful if you average the value based on their highs and lows.

Price guides give an appraised figure for each item. Because the prices may be determined from different bases, the variances between price guides and price lists seem confusing; yet all methods are helpful to both the professional and the amateur collector. For the serious collector, it is vital to keep abreast of the constant price changes of antiques and collectibles since values are constantly affected by inflation, acquisitions, and trends.

With collecting, some costs are intangible, such as the price of learning. Not so
intangible is the bottom line of acquiring reference books. For dealers, of course, it
is a business expense. For the average collector, however, it is simply an added cost.
In fact, it is possible to spend so much on a reference library, that you don't have
enough left to buy your collectibles. As Buck Hannon, a skilled purveyor of antique
facts and lore, said to me once: "The buyer of books should not be too impressed by
whether they are handsome. Sometimes the more modest publications contain the
best information." Plain or handsome, they are aplenty. For example, there are
probably more books on doll collecting than there are doll collectors. With so much
information available to help you become a true collector, ignorance is no longer
an excuse.

TAX GUIDELINES

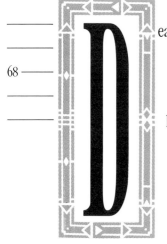

ealers are aware that it is necessary to keep accurate accounting records of their business transactions; they don't need me to tell them that. If they are not cognizant of tax guidelines, I am sure the IRS will enlighten them. For questions on good accounting procedures, it is best to retain professional assistance.

But what about the collector? Is it necessary to keep account of the buying and selling of collectibles? It certainly is. Let me explain why. Fine antiques that will appreciate in value certainly have a taxable basis; for example, suppose you buy a reclining Victorian chair *(Figure 18)* for $200 (which would be an incredible bargain for this rare piece). Later, your neighbor offers you $500 for it, and you decide to sell. Consequently, you have put yourself in a tax situation where that $300 profit is a reportable gain. Whether it is reportable under the basis of long-term capital gain or under current income would be determined by the tax laws at the time. In any case, though, there is reportable gain.

There are conflicting opinions regarding the tax liability when a person trades up rather than sells outright. If someone buys a Victorian sofa for $1,000 and later sells it for $1,500, clearly the tax liability is $500. If that same sofa is *traded* for one of higher value, is there a tax liability? Most professionals in collecting say no. My suggestion, in any questionable situation, is to get the opinion of a tax expert.

Obviously not everyone is keeping such records, and the IRS is unlikely to press the issue with collectors who occasionally trade or sell. Still, the bottom line is that no matter what the transaction you are responsible for tax reports.

24 | *Marble top*
mirrored chest

Sometimes you will hear antique dealers tout the purchase of antiques for a business office as a deductible business expense. If you check with the IRS, you will find that antiques used in a business are a write-off only if there is depreciation. So if you buy a fine partner's desk for $500, and the next year it is worth $600, there is no depreciation. Consequently, there is no business deduction.

Although it may be possible to go to certain branches of the IRS and get a written statement that allows some concession toward equipping an office with antiques rather than modern furniture, these exceptions are given on a very limited basis. No one should assume that "it is all tax deductible." Believe me, I have looked into it many times because my own office is decorated with antiques. I would love to have a tax write-off on the basis of my acquisitions, but, according to all I've been able to ascertain, it can't be done.

Granted, there are a few business items of a minor or necessary nature that are older (not necessarily antique), and therefore deductible. Any dated *equipment* that is depreciated in value but is still functional, would be an example.

Occasionally, I hear of people who decorate their office with art that they intend to claim as depreciation because the artist is "obscure." Perhaps they can do that if the IRS and the owner of the art agree on what is "obscure." To me, this also seems risky because even an "obscure" artist's work can appreciate in value.

Perhaps I am being too conservative on these tax issues. Maybe you can find room for more flexibility. But this is one of the few times I really agree with the IRS. Whether you agree or not, to decide to buy a major antique purchase solely because you assume it is a great write-off is not wise business. Either buy it just because you want it, or be sure it is deductible before you buy.

APPRAISALS

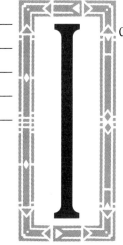

I don't think a person needs to be a member of a professional association of appraisers to be a good appraiser, but the certification and credentials certainly help. In my mind, there is great concern about appraisals that are done inexpertly, with the intent to secure the approval of the owner rather than to verify authenticity and value. Ultimately, that is not fair to the client. One protection against such abuse is to use an appraiser who is a member of a professional organization.

Some people will also put an appraiser on the spot for free advice. Generally, people will recognize that it would not be fair to a physician for someone at a party to come up and ask for an instant diagnosis. Similarly, an appraiser deserves to be compensated for his or her expertise.

With that in mind, let's look into what appraisers do, what they charge, and how to find a responsible one. Good resources for finding a reputable appraiser are local banks, art museums, or your general insurance agent. Your phone book may cite professional affiliations as well, which can also be helpful.

I happen to think a general insurance agent is one of the best sources for a good referral. Since almost all unusual antiques must be appraised before they can be insured and since insurance companies would never insure something without a competent appraisal, what better contact could you make to find an appraiser?

Most museums have a list of good appraisers, each of whom has his or her own specialty. Since museums will authenticate pieces but will not evaluate them, they keep such lists of "people of expertise" to whom they send owners of unusual or

26 | *Mica flecked*
Steuben candlesticks

27 | *Pressed glass cake compote*

valuable items. No one at the museum will ever discuss appraisal fees; this is between the individual appraiser and the client. The museum may have a range of appraisal fees that they are willing to recommend, but normally they will not enter into it beyond that.

Many antique dealers also recommend appraisers because they realize there can be a conflict of interest between appraising and being a dealer. I am sure most ethical dealers who do an appraisal feel bound by the same ethical principles dictated by professional appraisal associations: No appraisal will be made with the intent of immediate or later purchase by the appraiser or any agent of the appraiser.

If a seller takes an item to a dealer for evaluation, the following approach facilitates an honest transaction between the seller and the dealer. Ask the dealer, "I want to sell this, what will you give me for it?" Then you will be offered full value, and you can determine whether or not you want to accept the offer.

The upshot is that it is absolutely imperative to have your possessions evaluated before calling in a buyer. In case you doubt the necessity of taking this precaution, here is the quintessential tale of the sweet old lady who did not know any better: As the buyer she had called in took off in his truck with more than $10,000 worth of marketable antiques, this poor woman stood there very happily clutching the $1,000 he had paid her. Her beautiful Handel lamp alone was worth around $1,800. What galls me the most about this particular incident is the ploy the buyer used to secure that valuable lamp without paying the owner what it was worth.

I know the details of his exploit because he bragged to me about it, not knowing I was familiar with the situation. What he did when he saw the lamp was to pay very little attention to it until he was ready to leave. Then he said, "Oh, I don't know if we can use this lamp or not. It's not too bad, though, so I'll give you $5 for it and take it along with me."

It was certainly naive of the lady to just let her possessions go like that—and although such a larcenous manner begs for protection for the owner, practically speaking, it is up to the owner to see to that protection. In a case such as the one above, it would have been wise to have two or three people give bids. That way, the lady could have sold everything at once, and she would have been certain of a reasonable return.

Another option is to pay someone to determine fair market value before you put anything up for sale. Certainly, that is an added cost. But in every case I have seen, what the owner gains in the selling price far outweighs the appraiser's charge.

The next logical thing to discuss is appraisers' fees. Rule number one is: never pay an appraiser based on percentage of value. On that basis, it is too tempting for the appraiser to elevate values—and too often those values are inflated by 50 to 100 percent in order to bring about a substantial fee. For example, let's take an appraisal involving five pieces of period and Victorian furniture. If they are remarkable pieces, the appraisal value could easily reach $50,000; even at a 2 percent appraisal fee, the charge would be $1,000. So imagine the temptation to elevate the appraisal value for non-extraordinary items, perhaps even claiming a false authenticity for them. *(Figures 20, 22, 23, and 24).*

Most ethical appraisers charge on an hourly basis, with an extra fee for coming to your place of business or residence. The amount, however, can vary greatly. In the previous example, a certified appraiser should be able to give a complete description, including pictures, within a time frame of about one hour, for a cost to the seller of $75 to $100.

I must digress a bit here to point out that many of the major auction houses charge on a percentage basis for their appraisals. In view of their competence and the extra business costs, it seems fair to make them a partial exception to the rule with regard to this method of charging fees, especially if they refund the entire cost of the appraisal when the items are consigned to them for sale.

With extremely valuable items, a comprehensive written appraisal may entail additional research by outside experts. These appraisals can be costly. An example of such items would be fine works of art, where authenticity is absolutely vital.

If, however, the appraisal is just for general insurance purposes and the items are not of excessive value, then an appraisal for both the insured and the insurer can be written without too much time or money involved.

It is vital to discuss in advance with an appraiser the cost of a particular appraisal, the form of appraisal you need done, and how the appraiser plans to proceed. If there is no meeting of the minds after discussion, it is better to find a different appraiser.

My primary suggestion that the seller should get references is of utmost importance. If an appraiser comes well recommended and if you discuss your needs in advance, you will know the competence you can expect him or her to bring to the job.

Also, as I mentioned earlier, there are distinct advantages in having an appraisal done for insurance purposes. If items are on schedule or floater coverage or on a fine arts policy—and are covered by an appraisal—100 percent of the scheduled value will be paid to the owner in the event of loss. If, however, there is no such scheduled coverage backed up by an appraisal, the owner is bound by the extent of the homeowner insurance policy. This could have a considerably lower—and uncertain—value because of the lack of an evaluation before the loss. Once in a while, insurance companies allow some evaluation after loss, if sufficient evidence of value is available.

An example is the time a lady came to me almost in tears because her mother's spinning wheel had been stolen and the insurance company did not have the evaluation needed in order to make a settlement.

There seemed to be nothing other than a verbal description—and that verbal description gave the size of the wheel as anywhere from 18 to 40 inches, and the color of the wood as anywhere from honey oak to dark walnut. There was no mention of the condition of the wheel, whether it was intact with all its parts and in working condition; there was not even an indication of age. But the owner came up with a great solution.

A few days later—with her daughter—she came into my office carrying a projector with a reel of film. She set it up and showed me her home movie of the family Christmas party the year before. Her young daughter was playing in front of the tree, and just to her left was the spinning wheel. When the little girl stood up next to the wheel, it was possible to tell the size. I also determined the fact that it was a light honey oak—and even the condition of the wheel. With this appraisal, the woman was able to go to her insurance company, and they treated her very fairly. Obviously, she was a lucky lady, but we can't always depend on luck.

Another time, an insurance company called me to go out to a home that had been gutted by fire. The purpose of my visit was to see if I could find any of the items I had appraised some three years before. (I would counsel both appraiser and client to keep copies of their appraisals for at least five years.) I did have a copy of the appraisal, and on my list were items such as Goebel Hummel figures, Cloisonne, and Indian baskets. As we went through the list, the couple said, "Oh, that was destroyed, and we threw it out the upper window as we tried to clean things up."

True, there was a pile of debris outside the window, including black shards of various items, but I was concerned that they could not show me just one melted Hummell, or the shape of a Cloisonne piece—even if all the enamel had been burned out. Absolutely nothing seemed to be available. When I came to a beaded Indian dress and moccasins that were on my list, their response was the same—out the window in the clean-up.

At this point, I said, "I really don't think that is what happened, because you sold that dress and moccasins six months ago to a dealer who subsequently asked me to come out and reappraise it."

The blank and rather frightened looks on the faces of this young couple confirmed to me that they were endeavoring to make a dishonest claim with the insurance company. I left immediately and turned my report over to the company. It was not my job to follow up on the situation in any way beyond this, so I don't know what the insurance company did—whether they settled in part or at all. This was the first time I had ever personally come across anyone attempting such a deliberate misrepresentation or outright fraud, and I found myself totally appalled at the whole idea.

At the other end of the spectrum is the client who is somewhat naive about what items even need to be appraised. I believe an appraiser should always ask, "Do you have anything else I should look at that might be tucked away?" In my own experience, this has proven to be of vital importance to clients on more than one occasion.

I remember in particular one lady's response. "Well, not really. I just have a pair of candlesticks that I am going to give to a local charity."

With that, she reached back into the recesses of her china hutch and brought out a wrapped pair of 14-inch candlesticks—mica flecked, cintra style Steuben—that were as beautiful as any pair I have ever seen *(Figure 26)*. It just so happened that she didn't like them; but when I told her that their value was around $900, her thoughts about donating them to the local charity flew out the window.

I was sorry for the sake of the charity that would not get such a wonderful donation, as well as for the person who now would not find these treasures waiting to be discovered on a shelf somewhere. But I was not surprised to note that the owner's appreciation of those candlesticks seemed to be much greater when I left than when I had arrived.

Now, this is an example of a situation where the appraiser could be tempted to buy something from the customer—and would also feel tempted to lower the appraisal figure for his own benefit. Just as a dealer may sometimes face a conflict of interest when appraising, so may the private appraiser who sees something he or she wants very much. Should the appraiser ever buy on the spot? I feel, without equivocation, that the private appraiser should no more buy during an appraisal than should a dealer who is appraising. Appraising and buying—being in such direct conflict with each other—should be kept totally apart.

Very often, while I am appraising, an individual will ask me if I would like to buy a certain item I have especially appreciated. I think the only ethical response to that is, "Yes, I would. I will submit my written appraisal to you along with my bid, so you can check with other people. Then, should you desire to sell this later on, I will be happy to buy it at the bid figure." I believe this is fair to everyone. It makes certain that the appraiser gives the full value in writing; it states the bid figure that the appraiser is willing to pay; and it gives the owner time to see if he can obtain a better price. Then, if a transaction is completed later, it is done in a straightforward way without the built-in conflict of the appraiser-turned-buyer. My only quarrel is with anyone who buys an item immediately, or with someone who appraises with the intent to buy. This is certainly a conflict of interest, one that takes unfair advantage of the owner or seller—and it is blatantly unethical.

Perhaps this is a good time to differentiate between the various types of appraisals. I would group them in three general categories: 1) Appraisals for the purpose of buying or selling; 2) Appraisals for estates or conservatorships; 3) Appraisals for insurance. Taking these three categories one at a time, let's talk about appraisals for the purpose of buying or selling.

Let's assume that you have some fine Spode china *(Figure 25)* left to you by a relative. Let's further assume that you have no great appreciation for this inherited china. The logical step might be to sell it—perhaps to friends or relatives who like it and would be happy to buy it. Yet they don't know what to offer, and you are not sure what to ask.

Sometimes, there is an awkwardness in business dealings between friends, neighbors, acquaintances, or relatives. The best way to alleviate that awkwardness is to have someone who is objective place a value on your item. That way, if it is more than the amount your friends or relatives want to pay, they can be upset only with the outside party who evaluated the item. Yet you, the seller, can still come out looking good in their eyes. You even have the option of offering to sell it to them at a bit lower price than the appraised value. Then again, if your friends or relatives are not interested in purchasing your Spode china after an impartial appraisal sets things straight, maybe they didn't want it that badly in the first place.

Any appraiser hired for the purpose of determining values for buying or selling should have complete, current knowledge of the market for the items under consideration. A competent appraiser should be willing to admit when he or she is in doubt and take the time for further research. In this case, any added costs for extra time should be discussed and agreed on prior to spending the time. It is senseless to pay $30 for research on a pressed glass cake plate or compote *(Figure 27)* just because the appraiser wants to find out the exact pattern, and when and where it was made. If the appraiser can come within $5 to $10 of the value of that $40 cake plate or compote without added research (there are over five thousand pressed glass patterns), wouldn't it be better to just take an approximate figure?

If the item in question is a fine antique or any kind of artwork, the necessary time must be taken. I don't think anyone would mind paying a research fee to have someone determine if the work is an original by a recognized artist. I have experienced this in many instances.

Once, while I was doing appraisals at a charitable function, a lady came to me with a rolled-up canvas. As she smoothed it out, she watched me for a reaction. Well, she got it—because what she had was an original Norman Rockwell. Luckily, she was aware of it, and she proceeded to tell me the story behind her possessing this remarkable oil painting.

The Upjohn Corporation had hired Rockwell to do some advertising illustrations. Apparently, he did several sketches and a couple of oil paintings, before doing the final work that was used for the promotion. He then gave away the sketches and the preliminary oil paintings—one to a vice president of the corporation. The lady who had brought the painting to me for evaluation was the daughter of that lucky recipient.

I decided to proceed with caution in appraising this gem. After checking on current values, I came up with an evaluation of $20,000. Not bad, especially if you consider the fact that the painting had been rolled up in the back of a closet for many, many years.

Another time, while doing appraisals for an older couple, I noticed an interesting print on the wall. It was of a coast guard cutter in rough seas, and I recognized the artist as Sidney Laurence. I remarked casually, "I see you have an excellent print by Sidney Laurence."

The lady of the house said to me, "No, Mr. Rau, that isn't a print. That is an original painting by Sidney Laurence."

When I went to study it more closely with a magnifier, I discovered that it was indeed an original painting by this remarkable Alaskan artist. I knew immediately that it was the "mother lode" in an otherwise modest appraisal. The purpose of this particular appraisal was to be able to ease the budget during their retirement years, so I knew this was going to be a pleasant surprise.

I gave them the rough figure of "at least $25,000, and perhaps more." *Perhaps* turned out to be *definitely* because I found out after further research that it was a much-sought-after painting. The history of how it came into their hands was somewhat vague, but I'll never forget this unexpected find that more than merited some extra effort on my part.

A market can easily be manipulated by an opportunistic buyer. When this happens, values become skewed and much harder to predict. Unfortunately, this is a fact of life that doesn't seem likely to disappear— all the more reason for an appraiser to be alert for unexpected changes.

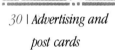

30 | Advertising and
post cards

Another form of appraisal is done for estate purposes. This type, generally done by referral through the courts or an attorney, requires a determination of the value at the time of the owner's death. In actuality, this translates as the value of an item in the case of a transaction between a willing buyer and a willing seller within a reasonable time after the death.

Obviously, the value will be lower with these time constraints than if time were allowed for repairing, restoring, and marketing the items for the best possible buyers. It is not a situation where it is possible to attach a high value and then wait for that price to be met. The courts and attorneys recognize these differences in value. Certainly, the appraiser should also be aware of the specific procedure and purpose.

Another type of appraisal is for conservatorship values. The purpose of this is basically what the word implies—to conserve as much value as possible. These evaluations are generally needed when an older person requires costly care and is incapable of determining values within his estate or of securing buyers at reasonable prices.

A conservator is usually appointed by the courts to determine values on an appraisal basis. In case liquidation becomes necessary, these appraisals serve as a guide for setting prices. Stated conservator values will be higher than estate appraisals since a conservatorship allows the time needed for disposition at sought-after prices.

Why must an estate be evaluated? Simply because it is required by law. There is a federal estate tax, and generally, a state inheritance tax, both based on value at the time of death. It is necessary when evaluating an estate to be fair both to the tax laws and to the estate itself in terms of value. A competent appraiser will understand the technicalities involved.

Finally, there is evaluation for insurance purposes—which means values of a realistic nature that are accepted by the insurance company for scheduling items or for floater coverages, with the realization that this is the probable cost of replacement of an item. It is important to remember that the insurer has the option of providing either the dollar amount or a replacement of the item. If a particular item can be replaced in near-identical form, the insurer will usually choose that option over replacement in dollars.

Some insurance appraisals are made with a slightly exaggerated nature, to cover the insured for the next year or two. However, if the appraisal is being done for charitable gift purposes, the IRS watches for exaggerated value. Should they suspect an inflated value, they appoint a panel of appraisers to determine an average figure, which will be the one used. If the original appraisal is a certain percentage above the IRS-determined value, both the owner and the appraiser are subject to severe penalty.

With items like silver or gold, trying to predict their future value is like trying to determine where a roller-coaster car will be at a given second—certainly difficult, maybe impossible. Although there are some appraisers who may claim to know everything about anything, in many cases you will want to consult with a specialist. Consider the intricacy of many treasured items, such as oriental rugs and tapestries, precious gems, *(Figure 28)* old silver, etc. Think of all the nuances involved in the three different types of appraisals. Then add to that the need to be completely aware at all times of the ever-changing marketplace, and you can appreciate the necessity to avoid the "jack of all trades and master of none."

With volatile values in certain items, it becomes increasingly difficult to appraise and insure—all the more reason to counsel patience, rather than the herd mentality one sometimes witnesses in times of financial upheaval. One needs to consider seriously whether it is really worth it to cash in that precious Tiffany bowl for a small percentage of its silver value (as I saw many people do in the early 1980s). Or is it more prudent to have it appraised, insure it at its full value, and then cherish it for its historical, rather than speculative, value? To keep or to sell—in either event, it is always best to know the value of your cherished items beforehand.

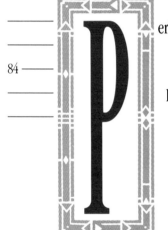

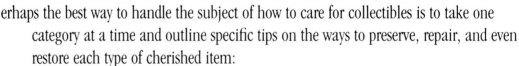

Perhaps the best way to handle the subject of how to care for collectibles is to take one category at a time and outline specific tips on the ways to preserve, repair, and even restore each type of cherished item:

Bronzes. The late Hamilton Aaris was a remarkable artist as well as a great friend of mine. Not only accomplished in his own artistry, he was the owner of some magnificent bronzes as well. I clearly recall his story about the day one of his young daughters tried to be helpful by polishing all the green patina off a three-foot bronze. She wanted to make it shiny for "Papa." When Hamilton came back from his studio that day and walked into the house, there was this gleaming bronze, certainly beautiful and decorative in nature, but now totally devoid of character. How could anyone possibly paddle a little girl who had tried so hard to do something nice? He did. Of course, that innocent lapse was soon forgotten, but it will take another thirty years for the patina to return. So don't ever try to clean off the natural patina on bronzes, brasses, or copperware. That patina is part of the character of the material. It is indicative of years of natural wear.

Clocks. Professional clock restorers often say that a clock can still be considered an original if no more than 30 percent of it is replaced or restored. I do not know if that includes the porcelain faces or the proper pendulums, weights, or glass doors, etc. I have never tried to do clock restoration myself—the only thing I ever did was to try to clean out the hardened grease and dirt of an old

31 | Mission-style clock

Mission-style clock *(Figure 31)* by using a solvent on its works. Unfortunately, I was not very successful in my endeavor; the spring was so tight and filled with grime it just would not come loose. Because of the delicacy of clock works, I would suggest leaving old clocks and watches to the professionals.

Cruets. *(Figure 33)*. I will give just one tip on caring for cruets: When you wash your cruets and put the stoppers back in, *keep them away from the window while they dry.* The sun, shining through the window, gives a "greenhouse effect," reacting on the trapped moisture in a way that can result in one of two things: either the stopper will pop out—and perhaps break—or the cruet itself will crack. It is so easy to forget this hint, but, tragically, I have seen this happen many times.

Furniture, parts replacement. If you are going to replace hinges, drawer pulls, escutcheon, etc.—and you want to maintain the integrity of your furniture— try to find original pieces. There are shops that carry both the originals and reproductions of the proper hardware. It seems completely incongruous to see a magnificent old pine cupboard still with its original doors—but with shiny brass hinges and Phillips screws. So, if you want to maintain as much of the original as possible, take the time to discover what type of handles or pulls were used, or how the escutcheons looked. It is well worth the effort, and how proud you will be of the authentic look you have managed to capture.

Furniture preservation. Fine furniture and fabrics, as well as rugs, quilts, and samplers, should be kept out of strong, continuous sunlight. Over time, the incessant sunlight will fade these fine things. Also for that reason, furniture and fabrics should be rotated to be kept out of persistent sunlight. If you have ever seen a fine Chickering piano that has been placed in direct sunlight for a period of time, take a look at what it does to the finish. It is certainly sad to see any fine furniture hurt by not being well cared for; one of the saddest is to see a Chickering "checkering."

Furniture restoration. If you are going to strip, refinish, or repair furniture, get a good book on the subject and study up first. Even proper stripping demands careful research. Some paints, oils, and stains penetrate the wood so deeply that stripping can be too obvious—so it is best to check with professionals with regard to this.

Glass, cameo. If you have a piece of Daum Nancy cameo that is slightly damaged because of acid cutback or hand decoration, you have a different story. Occasionally, a professional restorer can take a piece like this with a slight chip or flake and do some analogous enamel work in such a professional way that you will never notice it. So, if the purpose of restoration is to put things back visually into the original condition, you have accomplished your objective.

Let's face it, when many of these cameo pieces were first made, the acid
cutback and enameling covered flaws or errors in the blowing. So if you or a
restorer can do some artwork on a piece like this, go for it.

Glass, ceramic figurines. How about figurines of Meissen, Dresden, Hummel, or
other well-known ceramic and porcelain pieces? Let's say you have broken the
arm off a fine Meissen figurine *(Figure 29)*. This is an instance where you will
need a professional restorer, which you can find listed in the Yellow Pages. I have
seen arms and hands—including new fingers—restored so beautifully that you
could not see the work even with a magnifying glass. (Of course, repairs do show
up under black light.) Although repaired or restored pieces are of lesser value on the
market, to you, the value may not be diminished. Never try these tricky restorations
yourself, though; your repair may end up looking like a broken bone that was
never set properly.

Glass, cut, clear, pressed, or art glass. What should you do about your beautiful
cut-glass bowl that is cracked in two? You can look at it with dismay and say it
will never be the same—and you will be right. However, if you cherish it and
want to preserve it, then repair it. I am talking primarily about transparent,
cut, pressed, or art glass. These glass forms do not always require the attention
of professional restorers, because no matter how well a clear piece of glass is
repaired—even one with miter or pattern cut—the break will show. There is
a natural refraction in glass that will indicate the break; even a professional

restorer cannot avoid this. So, if you get a good clear-glass epoxy, mix it properly, and then glue the pieces together according to instructions, you may have a restoration that is perfectly acceptable. However, when it comes to grinding out chips, smoothing a surface, or imaginatively reshaping, by all means consult a professional.

Glass, general. Throughout this section, please keep in mind that I am referring to maintaining the integrity of a piece. If you decide to sell a restored piece, in all kindness pass that information on to the potential buyer. It will be appreciated, and it may not even affect the sale.

Glass, iridescent. If you have iridescent glass, it is a similar situation. There is no acceptable way of providing proper iridescence without heat—and reheating and re-iridescing is a difficult and dangerous game. Generally, it does not work well. However, suppose you have a nice Quesal compote *(Figure 34)* about four inches high with a pedestal base—and a chip is out of the pedestal. If the chip is less than one-quarter-inch deep, take it to a good restorer and have the chip

ground down and smoothed out. The pedestal will be slightly less in circumference, the chip will be gone, and the repair will not be obvious.

Paintings. It is wonderful to see what the cleaning of an oil painting does to enhance not only its color and brightness, but also your appreciation of it. You can check with most libraries, historical societies, and art museums for the names of conservators. Then you can find out their rates for cleaning and restoring. Cleaning is one thing—total restoration, another. It is a good idea to determine what the value of your painting is both before and after cleaning or restoration—or perhaps it will be just a matter of the subjective value to you. Beyond the need to clean and restore your paintings, there is an absolute necessity to keep them out of direct, persistent sunlight, as incessant sunlight will fade them, sometimes beyond reasonable restoration.

Paper. You could simply keep paper products such as postcards, advertising cards, *(Figure 30)* valentines, etc., in a box and look at them from time to time. Yet it is wonderful to use viewing books with glassine pages which allow you to insert the cards so they can be viewed front and back. Often the "message side" is just as fascinating as the artwork and design. Furthermore, the glassine preserves these fragile paper items in a way that will allow your grandchildren and great-grandchildren to see them in all of their glory fifty or a hundred years from now. If you don't take the time and care to store them properly, imagine how bedraggled, torn, and faded they will become.

Silver, quadruple-plate. If you have quadruple-plate table pieces dating back to the 1870s, you are going to have dark and dingy hollowware that appears almost pewterlike. You can have it replated, but shiny, new-looking 1870s silverware will look a bit out of place. Actually, the old pewter appearance is part of the charm, as it serves to document the obvious age of these items. However, this appearance does mean that the silver plating is pretty much gone. I have seen people work for hours on old, worn quadruple-plate, trying to repolish it, and all they manage to get out of it is a dull luster. Although in most cases replating is not recommended, certain items seem to demand it. If your flatware looks so dingy you are ashamed to display it or use it and you don't mind the bit of incongruity involved, then by all means, go ahead and have it replated. Or if you have an especially showy piece, such as a large tilt water on a stand with the goblet in the front, maybe replating would be a good idea. This is a very attractive item; if it is dull, replate it so you can show it off.

Silver, sterling. If your sterling silver becomes tarnished, the obvious thing to do is polish it. You don't need a professional for that. If there is some damage, maybe a professional restorer can refurbish it. You can be the judge of how important it is to you.

Stamps. If you have an old stamp collection, make certain the stamps are well protected in glassine holders, preferably the kind with a hinge on the back *(Figure 32)*. Old collections can be fun to preserve, besides providing an enjoyable way of getting into stamp collecting. Not only will you learn about stamps and how to keep them, but you will also learn how to preserve other paper products. Now, if the old stamps are glued into the books, all you have is a very interesting collection, with the value decreased considerably. One of the most important things about stamps is that they must be kept in a place where moisture cannot get to them. I recall seeing a beautiful old stamp collection some years ago that had been stored in cupboards above a washer/dryer unit. You can probably guess what had happened. Twenty sheets of old commemorative stamps were completely stuck together; they could not even be pulled apart for use as postage. That was certainly a sad case, but one that illustrates graphically how important it is to protect your stamps from moisture.

34 | *Quesal compote*

POTPOURRI

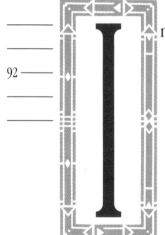

In my not so trivial pursuit of antiques and collectibles, I frequently run across interesting tidbits that we don't really need to know, but might just want to know. Hope you enjoy Potpourri.

Amberina. Amberina is often called "the glass with a golden touch." There are those who say that its transmuted tones, ranging from yellow at the base to deep red at the top, came about purely by accident. Legend has it that a workman accidentally dropped his gold ring into a batch of amber glass that was being blown. Whether or not that first batch was merely a stroke of luck for future collectors (but certainly not for the poor workman who lost his gold ring), amberina remains a consistent collectible.

The Armoire. The armoire first became popular during the reign of France's "Sun King," Louis XIV. It proved a handy place for the husband, returning from the Thirty Years War, to stash his mail. For the lady, it proved a handy place to stash her male, if said husband's return was unannounced. Modern collectors have found other uses for them. From liquor cabinets to compartments for electronic components, the armoire can always be put to good use.

Art Deco. At the turn of the century, European artists decided Art Nouveau was "too sweet" and replaced it with Art Deco, which can hardly be called sweet. In Art Deco, the lines are strongly directional. They may zig and zag to form geometric angles, but they certainly do not flow. Art Deco patterns are clearly symmetrical. If you draw a vertical line through the center of an Art Deco piece, the design on either side will be an identical mirror image of the one on the other side.

Art Nouveau. Art Nouveau once had among its many descriptive terms the one of "moderne"—a distinction that its design successor, Art Deco, quickly usurped. Originally, however, Art Nouveau was a relatively stark break from the florid Victorian era. Yet, within the ranks of Art Nouveau's founders, one renegade, Arthur Heygate Mackmurdo, broke from the movement's original direction toward simplicity. He introduced asymmetrical furniture and other items, all based on the free-flowing style of nature. Today, after various revivals, collectors seek out the early pieces, which are considered more valuable than the traditional ones on which Art Nouveau symbols were simply added.

Art Pottery. The first art pottery business is attributed to Maria Longworth Nichols. There were many ceramic manufacturers in the country in 1880, the year Mrs. Longworth got bored with being a housewife and asked her father to help her turn her hobby into a business. Her Rookwood factory, however, became the forerunner of ceramists devoted to art forms.

Aurene. The name Tiffany is synonymous with fine iridescent glass, so much so that the average person forgets how many keen competitors there were, although Tiffany himself rarely forgot. Among the first to challenge him was Frederick Carder, who produced the brilliantly hued Aurene glass at his Steuben glassworks. In fact, of all the innovations in art glass that are attributed to Frederick Carder, the creation of the dazzlingly iridescent Aurene probably best assures his fame. Aurene is actually a finish on glass, which has been demonstrated by the fact that the finish may be cut into (in the manner of cut glass), to produce a non-iridescent design. In sheer brilliance of color, Aurene can top all of its competitors. A piece of gold iridescent Tiffany, when set next to a piece of gold Aurene, appears muted by comparison. Unfortunately, not all Aurene is signed. However, the back catalogs of Steuben list almost every piece issued. Collectors can trace a piece they suspect to be Aurene through these catalogs.

Barbed Wire. Not all collectibles appeal to the aesthete. Barbed wire is one that has become a popular collectible since its original thorny presence in the Wild West. Also known as "Bob Wire" to many generations, the 18-inch pieces used for collecting (called "sticks") come in designs both simple and intricate.

Beer Cans. Another less-than-beautiful collectible is the beer can. The first beer to be sold in cans was a brand called Krueger, which was made in Richmond, Virginia. Its premier on January 24, 1935, was strictly experimental—and the rest is history.

Bohemian Glass. When glassmakers first set up shop in the Bohemian forests in the fifteenth century, what they produced was known as Waldglas. Its designs were largely influenced by the Venetian glassmakers who immigrated to the area. Not until the seventeenth century did the Bohemian glassmakers inaugurate their own brand of engraved glass, using diamond-point and wheel-engraving instruments. Many collectors today look for the glass of that period. Although there is no modern country of Bohemia, modern renditions of the namesake glass continue to be made. However, today's variety is of no great value to collectors.

Capo-Di-Monti. One of the acceptable occupations of kings during the eighteenth century was to become associated with the production of fine porcelains. In France, at the behest of Madame Pompadour, Louis XV acquired control of the porcelain factory at Sèvres. In Naples, King Charles established a porcelain factory, naming its product after the royal palace—Capo-Di-Monti. Modern-day collectors are bemused to discover that this particular royal factory became too common, when Charles of Naples became Charles III of Spain in 1759 and moved his factory to Buen Retiro. Furthermore, his son, Ferdinand IV, opened yet another Capo-Di-Monti factory back in Naples in 1771. Because other European factories have pirated both the Capo-Di-Monti patterns and the name, it is hard to guarantee the age of particular items.

Carved Glass. The first piece of carved glass is traced to 1 B.C., when a Roman artisan created a mythological scene on an amphora of several layers of different-colored glass. Acquired by Sir William Hamilton from a Naples dealer, the artifact eventually made its way to the British Museum via the Duke of Portland. Called the Portland Vase, this precursor to cameo glass suffered tragedy when a demented person shattered it.

The Cash Register. The cash register was supposedly invented by a saloon keeper by the name of James Ritty, who worried about the honesty of his bartenders. The first one was patented in 1879, but later, an improved one was the precursor to the National Cash Register Company. Ritty named his machine "Ritty's Incorruptible Cashier."

Celadon. Also the name of a character in a romantic novel published by Honore D'Urfee in 1610, Celadon is the anglicized name for the classic Oriental ceramic. Although some museum-quality pieces can be traced to 935 A.D., Celadon has been widely reproduced through the ages.

Christmas Cards. The first Christmas card ever issued was considered downright sinful by temperance groups: It depicted a rather sedate family toasting to good cheer. Those that were offended said the illustration promoted drunkenness and other anti-social behavior. Although that first one, issued in London in 1843, did not go unnoticed, two decades elapsed before the idea of a Christmas card really caught on.

Cinnabar. The term cinnabar is commonly misused to refer to all carved lacquer that comes from China. Cinnabar is only one of several coloring agents used to produce the different hues in carved lacquer.

Clocks, Grandfather. Antique clock fanciers often can be sticklers for nomenclature. The clock most of us refer to as the "grandfather" should really be called a "Long Case" clock if it originated in England, or a "Tall Case" clock if it originated in America.

Clocks, Travel. The first travel clock was introduced in the early nineteenth century by Abraham-Louis Breguet. They were known as "carriage clocks" or "officers' clocks" because they filled a major need for military officers. Yet, when Breguet found himself in the grips of war, it was a human, rather than mechanical stroke, that roused the Royalist Breguet to flee for his life. The famed revolutionist, Dr. Jean Paul Marat, gave him warning, thus saving him from the guillotine.

Cloisonne. Although Cloisonne is associated with the Orient, the truth is that Europeans introduced these elaborate objects. However, both the Chinese and the Japanese produced the art form more beautifully at less expense.

Commemorative Plates. The first commemorative plate was produced in 1895 by the Danish porcelain firm of Bing and Grondahl. It was called "The Frozen Window" and depicted a winter scene in honor of the Christmas season. It sold for fifty cents and is now valued upwards of $3,000.

Crystal. Although manufacturers of crystal have at times added color for special effect, purists insist that to truly merit the name "crystal," it should be absolutely colorless — or crystal clear.

Customized Shaving Mugs. Before World War I, home shaving with a straightedge razor was a task not to be taken lightly. Since the cost of entrusting it to a professional was negligible, it was an everyday habit for most gentlemen to stop in at the barber. Also common was the practice of having one's own customized shaving mug, which could be made of a variety of materials — perhaps in the finest porcelain or even sterling. Most, however, were distinguished primarily by the personal information with which they were engraved. These extremely collectible barber accessories are found in various forms. The "occupational mugs" decoratively depicted the owner's line of work. A simpler version was the standardized "gentleman's mug," to which the owner added his name upon purchase.

Cut Glass. The knowledge of how to cut patterns in glass dates to the days of the Pharaohs, but the heyday of cut glass was called "the brilliant period" — from 1876 until the beginning of World War I. Truly collectible cut glass comes from this period.

Depression Glass. To survive the Depression years, glassmakers produced glass they could sell for a few cents apiece. The Depression glass that resulted from their efforts was literally given away at times — as a premium to entice people to spend a whole quarter at the movie house, for example. Decades later, collectors got on the bandwagon begun by Hazel Marie Weatherman — who challenged them to acquire complete sets without paying much more than the original cost — and the value skyrocketed.

Doctor Dolls. There is some controversy surrounding the history of the "doctor dolls," the carved ivory nude figurines from China. The story has it that the figurines were used in the days of the Empire as medical intermediaries between Chinese physicians and ladies of the court who had fallen ill. According to the legend, the doctor would present the doll to the lady's maid, who would then have the lady describe on the doll where her symptoms were occurring. However, authorities on Oriental culture say that heads would have rolled if any doctor had dared to present a nude figurine to any lady of the court. It is possible that the story was invented to add to the dolls' exotic appeal to the European tourists. Another popular explanation is that the dolls were made and sold in port cities, where they were quite a risqué novelty to the Victorian foreigners who bought them.

Faberge. If you like to hunt for Easter eggs, this is where you might start. Russia's Peter Carl Faberge made only about fifty-seven of the jeweled, enameled eggs, and the whereabouts of some remain unknown. Supposedly, Faberge's fate was closely allied with the destiny of the Romanov Czars. Sure enough, when the revolution came, down went the value of Faberge. But, oh, how it has bounced back! All authenticated Faberge runs from about $1,500 for a cigarette case up to literally millions for the eggs.

Federal Furniture. After Independence in 1789, designers and cabinetmakers in America tended to turn away from making furniture in the traditional English ways. The style that emerged became known as American Federal and was popular until the beginning of the Victorian period around 1835. In actuality, this American Federal furniture was neither very American nor very different from the new wave of furniture that was developing in Europe. The English furniture of the Empire period was adorned with griffins and sphinxes and other Egyptian or Roman motifs; American furniture substituted eagles, the

Union plaque, lyres, lions' paws and other carvings of less Imperial design. Federal fits in well with contemporary and traditional settings.

Gaudy Ceramics. Gaudy ceramics (Gaudy Dutch, Gaudy Ironstone, and Gaudy Welsh) are so called because of their bright colors. Because Gaudy ceramics were considered déclassé compared to their elegant porcelain relatives, the term was a put-down for the Pennsylvania Dutch who preferred it to other pottery. They had the last laugh, however, since Gaudy Dutch in particular is now a highly valued collectible.

Georgian Furniture and Silver. When collectors talk of Georgian furniture or silver, they are referring to a period that spanned some one hundred fifteen years—encompassing the reigns of George I, II, III, and IV.

Girandole. The catchall term for Victorian elegance, "Girandole," has its origin in referring to fireworks and the rotating jets of water in classical fountains. In short, it connotes something showy—whether that be sconces, brackets, candelabra, candlesticks, or jewelry.

Graniteware. Graniteware is both plentiful and collectible. In actuality, it is an enamel ware, and some of the older pieces—with pewter trim, handles, and lids—are rapidly growing in value. Colors were not limited to gray; it appeared in colorful swirled and mottled designs, as well as solid colors. In fact, apparently more of the graniteware was produced in solid white than in any other color. Many collectors fail to realize this and sometimes pass it by. Today, there is also a very beautiful, colorful graniteware being made in Yugoslavia and Mexico. Fortunately—and thankfully—it is so marked. Nevertheless, it, too, is quite collectible and undoubtedly will increase in value in the future.

Heisey's Animals. Although the Heisey Glass Company was founded in 1897, it did not begin to manufacture the crystal menagerie until about 1936. While most of the animals were in clear crystal, there were a few made in amber, flamingo, or in pale and dark cobalt blue. These colored ones are rare, and even the crystal is not inexpensive. Apparently they are not all marked; at least, the marking seems to have been haphazard. If they are marked, you will recognize the H within a diamond; but even if not marked, the knowledgeable collector finds that the Heisey Animals are easy to recognize—it just takes a little study.

Imari. As a general rule, Imari features a standard medallion in the center surrounded by six panels, each with symbolic decorations. There is a wide variety of Imari, and collectors sometimes classify it in a very confusing way: old Imari as opposed to old, old Imari, and brand new Imari as opposed to new Imari. Imari is now found in gift shops, and as you can well imagine, this is the brand new Imari. Most of these porcelains are from the Japanese Province of Hizen and take their name from the village of Imari. Buck Hannon stated that this was sort of an assembly point from which these interesting pieces were transshipped to Nagasaki for distribution throughout the world.

Imperial Stretch Art Glass. The type of Imperial art glass that has been dubbed "stretch" is so called because the finish of the glass has an onionskin appearance, which makes it look as if it were stretched over the basic shape of the piece.

Made in Occupied Japan. Exports made in Japan from the time of their 1945 surrender to the end of military occupation in 1952 were supposed to carry the stamp, "Made in Occupied Japan." Although General MacArthur pressured manufacturers to do so, it was not mandatory. Stamp or no stamp, one defiant manufacturer had the last word in a more subtle way. Its toby mug—bearing a striking resemblance to MacArthur—commands a higher price as a collectible than other toby mugs marked "Made in Occupied Japan."

The Night Light. The first version of what is now known as a night light was the fairy lamp invented by Samuel Clarke in the nineteenth century. Even the advent of electricity could not extinguish the appeal of this quaint design. The popular Art Nouveau Nautilus lamp was made by Tiffany at the turn-of-the-century; that lamp and various other offshoots, are all in homage to the delightful, candle-powered fairy lamp.

Oriental Art. Oriental art is intended to convey meaning as well as aesthetics. Among the symbolic imagery is the dragon, representing power for the purposes of good; ducks in pairs, representing conjugal bliss; and the pine tree, peach, and the crane, all representing longevity. A complete study of the symbolism in Oriental art could take a lifetime, but a little knowledge is necessary in tracing antiques to their origin.

Pressed Glass or Pattern Glass. The pressed or "pattern" glass made in the 1800s could be considered the original "depression" glass. It, too, was in reaction to an economic depression (1836-1840), and pressing machines and molds were developed to produce dinnerware as efficiently as possible. The innovation of fire polishing also came about at this time. The reheating of pressed glass obliterated the marks of molds and tooling, giving the appearance of much finer glassmaking techniques.

Quezal and Durand Glass. Although Carder annoyed Tiffany to the point where he instituted litigation against him for infringement of patents, an upstart Tiffany employee named Martin Bach, Sr., made the excitable Tiffany almost apoplectic. Bach had been trusted, and when he left not only did he take with him many Tiffany designs and "secrets," but he also influenced other Tiffany workers to leave as well. Bach's version of treasured art glass was named Quezal. The Bach defection passed on to the next generation, when Bach, Jr., went to help a Victor Durand of the Vineland Flint Glass Company create fine art glass, called Durand.

Railroad Date Nails. Generally, it is thought that these nails were made between 1900 and the 1930s. Their purpose, a very modest and straightforward one, was to determine the best woods and preservatives which could be used for railroad ties. When these ties were installed, a nail was driven into them with special coding on the head of the nail—the last two numbers of the year in which the ties were installed and a letter. If the letter "P" was used on the nail, it meant pine; "A" meant Ash. So there were designations for the various woods. Then when these ties were replaced because of deterioration, the railroads were able to determine which woods lasted longest in the various climates. The various railroads completed their research, and the nails were not used for identification after the late 1930s.

Reverse Glass Painting. Reverse painting on glass was quite the rage in the eighteenth and early nineteenth centuries. Since few artists of note were inclined to this form of painting, it became the arena of amateurs. However, the popular style was not easy, so a "cheater" device was dreamed up: A transfer outline was first impressed upon the back of the glass, leaving a pattern to fill in fairly simply. Amateur or no, the good reverse glass paintings were not done this way.

Rocking Chairs. Typically an American product, most rocking chairs were produced in the eighteenth century in the New England states, so the association with the characteristically plain Shaker Furniture is a very natural one. Whether it be a Boston Rocker or a Hitchcock Chair, we can safely call it "comfortable seating." Antique collectors and enthusiasts have rediscovered rocking chairs in every style and from every period of the past in which they were made. John Kennedy even brought his rocker to the Oval Office of the White House, thus creating for them the designation "decision makers." The early ones made of birch or maple probably retailed for $1.50. Now, depending on the ornateness and age, one hundred dollars would be cheap—and the price goes on up from there.

The Rolltop Desk. The 1890 advertisement heralding the appearance of the first rolltop desk declared it a "genuine anti-swear desk," because it had a place for everything. Businesses, however, swore by its innovative design, and it quickly became a standard piece of office equipment.

Scarab Design. The Egyptians have set the tone for collectible objects throughout the ages. Tiffany first got the bug more than fifty years before the discovery of King Tut's tomb kindled worldwide interest in Egyptology. What interested Tiffany was the jewelry made of reproductions of the Egyptian beetle, called a scarab. Back home, he created his own version of this ancient symbol in Favrile glass and in jewelry. The scarab and other Egyptian motifs continued to turn up in Tiffany works.

Snuff Bottles. Have you seen how "tough guys" sometimes roll a cigarette pack in their tee-shirt sleeve? How surprised they would be if they knew that the fad was started during China's Ch'ing dynasty. When the Emperor took up snuff, the Imperial Court followed suit, although the court costume, with no pockets, was not suited for the habit. To solve this problem, the delicately carved containers were fitted snugly into garment sleeves.

Steuben Glass. The Steuben Glassworks is the only "great" that survived the Depression, although Quezal, Durand, and Tiffany (of course) remain well-known names along with it. Since modern Steuben is generally clear crystal, it is sometimes forgotten that its founders once brought forth a plethora of richly colored glass.

Stradivarius Violins. "The great are always imitated" is a statement that applies as well to the greatest of crafted objects as it does to famous individuals. Although experts have accounted for all of the Stradivarius violins that were ever made, there are many people who erroneously believe they have a rare and valuable Strad that has been passed down through the family. The reason it is such a common occurrence is that twice in American history—once at the turn-of-the-century, and again during the Depression—some enterprising souls peddled tens of thousands of these ersatz Stradivarius violins across rural America. The spurious labels and the sales pitch (of grandfather having been a famed violinist in Europe) were equally convincing—and people bought both the story and the violins. Although they are imitation, in many cases the instruments are actually quite good. So if a traveling salesman pulled some strings with your ancestors, console yourself that you more than likely at least have a fine instrument, if not a genuine Stradivarius.

Teapots. When Europeans finally got around to tea drinking, about one thousand years after the Chinese had developed a taste for it, the pots they made emulated the Oriental style—without handles. However, the Europeans pre-ferred a warmer brew, so handles were developed. Also, since tea was expensive when first introduced in Europe, those early pots were made quite small—usually only large enough for a single cup.

Tiffany. As a man, Louis Comfort Tiffany was quite an eccentric. Flamboyant, exuberant, never the calmest man in a time of crisis, nevertheless, Tiffany was a genius in his field. Zealously possessive of his Nouveau style, he resisted all change and therefore hated Art Deco. Although most collectors think of Tiffany in terms of his magnificent glass and bronze, he is also known for manufacturing fine furniture, art pottery, and even jewelry. However, in his lifetime, all of these were merely an adjunct to his decorating business. As a fashionable interior designer for wealthy people, he amassed a great fortune. He lived lavishly, which is fitting with the now-lavish appreciation of his art.

Toby Jugs. Since the time of the ancient Egyptians, potters have produced jugs which depict famous figures. They eventually became known as toby mugs, or character mugs.

Venetian Blown Glass. Since the eleventh century, Venetians have been making fine art glass. By the late thirteenth century, however, Venetian glass blowers were exiled to the Isle of Murano (just off the coast of Venice). The supposed reasons for this move were to avoid the fire hazards that the numerous furnaces presented and to enforce better security against theft by workers. In fact, though, it was really an attempt to protect what was basically considered a state secret. Glassmaking was a state-owned monopoly: the government felt it would be easier to keep their fine techniques secret if the workers were isolated.

The Victorian Balloon-back Chair. In the late eighteenth century, the brothers Montgolfier invented the hot-air balloon. Its immense popularity carried over to everyday life, resulting in the appearance around 1840 of the Victorian balloon-back chair.

Watches. In their ornamentation and craftsmanship, watches represent a source of great pride—not only to the master artisans who created them and the skilled craftsmen who keep them running but also to the owners of these fine collectibles. Made of the finest of metals and jewels, these beautiful old pieces have a special place in the timeless order of collecting.

Waterford Crystal. True Waterford crystal is a relative newcomer, created after World War II. Although many of its patterns are based on older designs, the older glass was made not only in Waterford, but in other areas of Ireland.

Weapons. The subject of weapons is an extremely wide category and a fascinating field. Of course, the collecting of weapons is not for everyone; firearm collectors are a special breed. They know their weapons from the grip to the end of the barrel (thank goodness), from black powder to cartridges, from pistols to revolvers, shotguns to rifles. Weapons collectors "aim to please"—and to know their subject—regardless of the specific area of their expertise.

AFTERWORD

Well, I have always been told to end a presentation on a high note, and I think this is the time to do it.

If you collect simply for the love of collectibles — just for the pleasure of owning fine things — the price you are willing to pay for an item you want and the amount you can afford are your only true guides to what is a reasonable cost.

If, on the other hand, you are accumulating and searching for antiques or other collectibles for profit, you will certainly want to aim to buy low and sell high. Remember that collectible values, like stock market figures, are somewhat cyclic — in fact, even fickle. In just a few short years, Beam and Avon bottles have gone from very high to very low in value; conversely, some pieces of Carnival and Depression glass have moved from very low to very high. Naturally, we all like to see the value of our collected items increase, but part of the appreciation and even the value to us has to be in our own pure enjoyment of collecting and the knowledge that we are helping to preserve our wonderful heritage.

It is a never-ending thrill — and it is a real thrill — to have collectors come up and say, "love your show." This has never been a bother. Collectors, like the varied items they collect, are such fascinating people they never lack for a topic of conversation. It seems that we collectors have so much to talk about, and the search for nostalgia is such a cooperative effort involving all of us, that we never truly meet a stranger. Collecting is the heartbeat of the past, the drumbeat we march to in the present, and the echo of the future.

INDEX

103